THE RIVER BEAT

First published 1997
by Historical Publications Ltd
32 Ellington Street, London N7 8PL
(Tel: 0171-607 1628)

ISBN 0 948667 41 9
British Library Cataloguing-in-Publication Data
A catalogue record for this book is available from the British Library

Typeset in Palatino by Historical Publications Ltd
Reproduction by G & J Graphics, London EC2
Printed by Edelvives in Zaragoza, Spain

Illustrations

With the exception of the portrait of Sir Paul Condon,
the illustrations in this book were kindly supplied by the
Thames Police Association at the Thames Police Museum,
98-100 Wapping High Street, E1 9NE.
The Museum is open to the public by arrangement.

THE RIVER BEAT

*the story of
London's River Police
since 1798*

by Geoffrey Budworth

with a foreword by
Sir Paul Condon Q.P.M.
Commissioner of Police of the Metropolis

HISTORICAL PUBLICATIONS LTD

Contents

Acknowledgements

River policing was, at the start, all done from Wapping and my narrative focuses on the divisional headquarters there, with a reference only now and then to the other later Stations. This is not to favour the men and women at Wapping or to overlook those officers downriver at Blackwall and Erith, at Waterloo Pier and Barnes, or 'up-along' at Hampton and Shepperton; it is simply to keep the book within limits.

Someone else would tell the story differently, recalling other events, characters and anecdotes. A lot happened in 200 years. This is my interpretation.

I purposely use the pronoun 'it' for a boat or ship, because 'she' is the seaman's term not always used by river boat crews who spend more time ashore than afloat.

I am grateful to The Commissioner of Police of the Metropolis, Sir Paul Condon, Q.P.M. for allowing this account of one of his Divisions, and for kindly writing a Foreword to this book. I would also like to thank the following: Divisional Chief Superintendent Phil Gaisford; Chief Inspectors Clive Chapman and Tom Pine; Chief Superintendent Alan Moss; the staff in the Directorate of Public Affairs at New Scotland Yard, who encouraged and helped with the publication of this book; Inspector Phil Johns who updated me on the Underwater Search Unit which he led; John Joslin, a past-curator of the Thames Police Museum, without whose own research I could not have written much of this book; his successors, Danny Lines and Keith Gotch, for their knowledge and access to their archives; Peter Andrews, editor of the *Thames Police Association Journal*, for material from its numerous issues as well as his invaluable help and guidance; Ms A.E. Duffield at the Imperial War Museum and Christine Reynolds, Assistant Keeper of the Muniment Room and Library at Westminster Abbey, for information concerning Patrick Colquhoun; the Revd Fred W.B. Kenny, M.A., H. Dip. Ed., Rector of Stambridge parish church, Essex, in which churchyard the remains of John Harriott rest.

Sir Paul Condon, Q.P.M.
Commissioner of Police of the Metropolis

Foreword

by Sir Paul Condon Q.P.M.
Commissioner of Police of the Metropolis

This excellent book is about policing on the River Thames. I am delighted that Geoffrey Budworth has written it because, like many other excellent British institutions, Thames Division does its work quietly, with many aspects of professional achievement not otherwise obvious to public view. We have needed a champion to tell the story.

There are many graphic accounts in these pages, not least the stories about the first heroes who started the Marine Police Force more than thirty years before the Metropolitan Police was formed. It was therefore the first organised modern police force in this country. Those first officers had no police tradition to guide them, but they did have the enormous and daunting challange of combatting wholesale theft, corruption and lawlessness in what was, in the 1790s, the wealthiest trading port in the world where 1700 ships might be accommodated at any one time. Crime was cut very dramatically.

In the first few months their headquarters was besieged by a rioting mob intent on freeing three prisoners and smashing the court house. Shots were fired when the magistrates faced the mob to read the Riot Act, and Gabriel Franks was killed on duty. Heavily outnumbered, the police drove off the rioters, but not without use of firearms and killing a rioter.

The leadership, courage and wisdom of Patrick Colquhoun and the under-estimated John Harriott is a tale in itself. These two men deserve our gratitude for their unique contribution to the development of the British style of policing which has become so famous world wide. Their example must have influenced my own predecessors in the early days of the Metropolitan Police.

The River Thames has seen its share of pageants, but also tragedies. The *Princess Alice* was sunk in 1867 with the loss of over 600 lives; more recently the incident involving the *Marchioness* reminds us of the terrible dangers which can occur on the river and the need for emergency services to react quickly on the water.

The bi-centenary of Thames Division in 1998 is a good time to remember the fine history of past heroes, but also to look forward. The river is still significant in terms of London trade. The modern Thames Division continues to react to today's realities and will have a significant role in relation to safety on the river, responding quickly to emergencies and combatting a whole spectrum of crime for many years to come.

P.L. Condon

Preamble

To combat thieves and pirates in the Port of London, two resolute reformers teamed up in 1798 and founded a Marine Police Force. The same two men – magistrate Patrick Colquhoun and John Harriott, Master Mariner – were appointed by the West India Merchants & Planters to safeguard the valuable cargoes aboard their company's ships, and they and their hand-picked watermen imposed order in place of anarchy. Thirty one years later Robert Peel modelled his 'New Police' upon them and ten years after that, in 1839, the Marine Police were merged with the Metropolitan Police and became their Thames Division. Despite the merger, Thames Division has remained very much a separate entity and that is why the modern Thames Police Association chose for its motto *Primus omnium* (First of all) – they are the world's oldest police force, and in 1998 they celebrate their bicentenary.

The riches of the British Empire were once shipped to London's overflowing warehouses but World War Two bombing destroyed some of the buildings and industrial decline or social change emptied the rest. The river scene is different now but the work of the River Police is still as vital as it was when Charles Dickens visited and wrote about them.

The men and women of Thames Division today watch over 54 miles of historic waterway, patrolling day and night from Staines Bridge in Middlesex, downriver past the Houses of Parliament and the Tower of London, to Dartford Creek in Kent. Fast fibreglass diesel launches with centrally-heated cabins, two-way radios and flashing blue lights have replaced the original open rowing galleys made of English oak, and the dragging unit (a boat's crew blindly trawling the river-bed with grapnel hooks or strong magnets on ropes) is now a seek-and-search team of police frogmen.

The modern existence and capabilities of Thames Division were dramatically highlighted by a single incident in 1989. On 20 August that year, the Thames pleasure boat *Marchioness* was cruising in bright moonlight below Southwark Bridge on a City stretch of the river known as King's Reach. Aboard, a party of photographic models, their agents and friends were enjoying a weekend disco. It was Sunday morning at almost 1.50am when the empty gravel suction-dredger *Bowbelle*, outward bound downriver from Nine Elms and punching into the flood

1. Wapping waterside c.1900, overlooked by the second Thames Police H.Q.

*2. A Victorian blue lamp and a modern sign identify the Thames Police H.Q. at
98-100 Wapping High Street.*

tide, emerged from the central arch of the bridge. She rammed the party boat
with the mass of 1,475 gross registered tonnes multiplied by her speed. The
Marchioness was broken open, then overturned and, pushed under by the ship's
blunt bow, it sank in seconds. People on the upper deck were thrown into the
water or simply floated free; 24 passengers and crew were trapped and went
down with it to the riverbed where they drowned, while others succumbed before
help could reach them. A total of 51 died in the worst river accident this century.

Emergency services and news reporters learned of the accident and raced
to the scene. Seven officers of Scotland Yard's Thames Division (London's River
Police), blue lights flashing atop the white cabins of five powerful black-hulled
duty boats, used searchlights to find drifting survivors and hauled 53 of the
87 shocked and shivering survivors from the dark, fast-flowing tidal waters.
The motor vessel *Hurlingham* rescued another 34.

The occurrence was classified a 'Major Incident' by the authorities and special
contingency plans were put into operation. At 3.15 p.m. that afternoon the Prime
Minister, the Rt. Hon. Margaret Thatcher, was taken in the Police Commissioner's green launch to survey the scene. Later the same day the *Marchioness* was
raised from the bottom of the river by a Port of London Authority salvage vessel
and the lifeless bodies were taken from its interior. A mortuary was set up

in the disused basement boat repair workshop at the Thames Divisional Head-quarters, 98-100 Wapping High Street, to lay out the deceased for identification by relatives and friends, Policemen and women were drafted in from the Airport Division at Heathrow to staff this sad place, freeing Thames officers for grislier work afloat. In the next five days the River Police, working 12-hour shifts, recovered another 27 decomposing corpses from the river.

A police station has stood on that same riverside site in Wapping High Street, a few boat lengths upstream from the site of Execution Dock, for 200 years. The latest, built in 1908, is the third and it is an historic listed building. River guides on passenger launches point it out to sightseers; but it is also Thames Division's operational headquarters, from which boats go out on routine patrols and respond to emergencies. The building's symmetrical brick frontage, with its quoins and sills of hard white stone, faces the river, while the less imposing elevation seen by passers-by on the road is in fact the rear of the premises.

An earlier Victorian station dating from 1869 was narrower, but the same alleyway of flagstones ran beside it to foreshore steps, the public entrance then – as now – beneath a traditional blue lamp with its Imperial crown and the words 'Metropolitan Police'. An unnamed writer for the *Boy's Own Paper* who visited at the turn of the century reported that it was:

> '... a pleasant place, the Inspector's office with its bow windows looking out upon and up and down the river; but the dock and cutlasses ranged on the walls in geometrical patterns, and the handcuffs, give it an umistakeable air of business.'

This replaced the original structure, a converted dwelling house, which was falling apart and overrrun with rats when it was finally demolished. Charles Dickens had been there in 1853 and he noted the old Court room with its cabin-like windows looking onto the river, modified by then into a quaint charge-room containing a stuffed cat in a glass case and a portrait of a rare old Thames officer. This was Mr. Evans, who had been Chief Surveyor of the Marine Police for 18 years, prior to amalgamation, after which he served a further nine years as Thames Division's first Superintendent. When, at the end of the eighteenth century, the West India Merchants & Planters established Colquhoun and Harriott in "a spacious Police Office", it was this house (then 259 Wapping New Stairs) that they leased from the occupier, Samuel Turner, Esq. and his landlord, the Bridewell Hospital. They chose it because it was on the north shore, at the centre of the quays where most of the company's ships loaded and unloaded. It cost them just £832.6s.10d for an initial eight years.

Part I

CHAPTER ONE

Crime Scene

"...the River Thames was without a single Police Guard-boat,
and no antidote existed against the dangers..." (Patrick Colquhoun)

A ship's captain entering the Thames Estuary in the 1790s and sailing upriver to London was heading for the wealthiest trading port in the world: more than three quarters of Britain's merchandise, worth £75 million each year, passed in and out of the Port of London. Trade quadrupled during the eighteenth century; cargo ships doubled in size and there were twice as many of them. They brought to Britain the treasure and consumables of a growing empire of colonies that would, in the coming century, extend from India to the Americas. Her fishing fleets ranged from the Arctic to the Antarctic. Outward-bound went goods made in Britain (such as textiles); and, for every foreign-going British vessel, two more coasted in home waters. Through London's river came and went an extraordinary assortment of valuable commodities: cocoa; paving stones; cast iron; oak bark; calico; damask; linen; muslin; wool and other fabrics; wax and tallow; elephants' teeth and tusks; wine, brandy, gin, beer and cider; furs and skins; hosiery; corn and flour; ashes; seeds; whalebone, fins and blubber; cheese, salt, fish, butter and fruit; pitch and tar; cork, deal and hardwoods; smalts; snuff; drugs and dyestuffs – and many others.

But the Port was lawless. It was everyone's common law duty to protect life and property, and yet it was nobody's job. River workers connived with ships' officers to pilfer from cargoes or covertly looted them wholesale. And what could not be had by stealth was openly carried off by armed gangs. Over 36,000 individuals had a hand in discharging and loading ships, one in three of whom took whatever he or she wanted. A well-guarded vessel might escape untouched but many lost up to half their merchandise before it could be got ashore to owners and buyers. The Crown was also deprived of £500,000 a year in lost revenue.

As many as 700 junior Customs officers were corrupt. When one of them boarded an incoming vessel at Gravesend – then merely a village in Kent – he would suggest to the ship's mate that they could take and sell part of the cargo. If the ship was a frequent trader they may have done it before, although even a stranger would reason that with a revenue officer involved there could be little risk. Once the ship was anchored, moored or berthed, criminal receivers brazenly came aboard and valued the goods to be stolen. They provided the

3. The Thames looking downstream past St Paul's down to the old London Bridge.
This scene of crowded shipping was published in 1750.

necessary tools and containers: crowbars, adzes and shovels; sacks for sugar or spices; a tin tube with bellows that assembled into a pump (called a jigger) used to siphon rum from casks into bladders. They also paid the ships' officers and Customs men, often 20 to 30 guineas each, a year's wage for a few hours neglect of duty.

Thieving began about midnight with watermen, coopers and lumpers (dockers), each with a role. The muscular lumpers unstowed the heavy casks; coopers skilfully removed, and later replaced, the cask heads. All shovelled tea, coffee, ginger, pimento or whatever into big sacks, able to hold 100 pounds each, which were dyed black so that they could not easily be seen at night in the bottom of a waterman's wherry. Crooked watermen took turns to ferry loads ashore to the receivers in boats also often stolen for the enterprise. As one left a ship's side, another took its place, with secret (frequently changed) recognition signals used as a precaution against being caught unawares. In this way as much as 10-15 tons of sugar could be shifted before daybreak, netting them perhaps £200 in one night.

The plunder by these gangs, known as 'light horsemen', was enormous. In March 1794 a ship lost 50 tons through a conspiracy by the mate with five revenue officers and a notorious receiver. Ten hogsheads (large casks, each over 50 gallons capacity) were completely emptied and afterwards stowed in a part of the ship that leaked badly to give the impression that the sugar had been washed out during the voyage from Jamaica. The insurers duly settled. The same ship also lost three whole puncheons of rum, amounting to about 300 gallons, and another 300 gallons were pumped from different casks and sent ashore in skins and bladders. Coffee, too, was taken. The five Customs men shared £150. In August the previous year an East India Company merchant ship from Bengal lost large quantities of pepper, rice and 60 dozen bottles. Twenty-six officers shared the proceeds of that sale. And in November 1795, a China ship lying at Blackwall was plundered of 35 large tea chests by 37 Revenue officers and lightermen.

Crime bred crime. Daytime lumpers, who knew of overnight theft involving ships' officers, demanded freedom to pilfer as their price for keeping quiet about it. Each wore a waist band with secret pouches and wide-legged trousers with long pockets that could be filled with sugar, etc. These lumpers also took copper, brass and lead fittings, and utensils of all kinds, under a long coat to conceal any tell-tale bulges. But even these strong men must have found it hard to walk with the loads they carried off – no wonder they were nicknamed 'heavy horsemen'.

Thieves were everywhere. While one alert captain was on deck, searching dock workers he had discovered stealing cargo, a barrel of his own sugar was emptied into bags and dropped out of his cabin window. Below in a boat lay a waterman to catch them. He got away and the master only discovered his loss later.

Every trade had its tricks. About 400 journeymen coopers worked on board ships in the Port, repairing casks and crates. These craftsmen were allowed perks – such as cargo spilt from broken containers – but they broached intact ones, making the damage look accidental. Then, not only did they claim the contents, they charged for repairing the broken casks. Official and bogus ratcatchers roamed between decks with endless opportunities to steal. They also freed rats (previously caught and paid for on other ships) aboard clean vessels; then they laid traps for them and began all over again. Beset and betrayed, an infrequent trader had no chance. In August 1794 the captain of a small vessel from Antigua, in London for the first time, told Customs he was worried about the dock workers. The revenue men offered to discharge his cargo themselves and, reassured, he went ashore, whereupon they took five of his 70 hogsheads of sugar (seven percent of the cargo).

Receivers caused and paid for almost all of this villainy. Many were mere opportunists, traders willing to take and sell goods of uncertain origin from their handcarts, market stalls or shops. Some arranged crimes and forced others to do them, like the publicans and brothel-keepers who allowed regulars their pleasures on credit, then insisted upon repayment in stolen goods. Further indulgence was then permitted, at a fraction of the property's real value, and so it continued. About twenty receivers had grown rich and powerful. At the Old Bailey in 1797 it was revealed that one nearby City firm traded solely in stolen sugar, keeping at least one refinery in business. Some rope and twine manufacturers, too, relied upon stolen hemp, flax and cotton for raw materials.

How could larceny be so rife when the penalty was the treadmill, a prison hulk or death? By the late 1700s there were over 200 capital offences, including shoplifting goods valued at more than five shillings and pick-pocketing more than one shilling (the equivalent of only a few pounds today). Because judges and juries were reluctant to use such savage laws, however, few offenders were convicted of major crimes. Courts knowingly accepted evidence which under-valued property, so as to convert grand larceny (a hanging matter) into petty theft. In London and Middlesex, each year, just sixty were sentenced to death, and only twenty of them were hanged: mercy and pardons were readily granted to the others – and widely publicised. Nevertheless, because a thief risked execution or transportation with hard labour for life in a penal colony, otherwise honest officials might turn a blind eye for a friend caught in the act. In November 1796 an East Indiaman was discharging at Blackwall and, with the knowledge of the ship's officers, a quantity of shawls were taken from the cargo. These were hidden in casks, the ends of which were then stuffed with spunyarn and oakum (shredded old rope used to waterproof boats' hulls and deck seams) to appear as if these were their only contents. But an examiner who opened and probed one of them found the shawls inside. A port surveyor, friendly with the officers, heard of their predicament and rushed over to somehow square the official who then let the other casks go ashore unexamined. So corruption spread. Two men, however, were planning to stop it.

CHAPTER TWO

Colquhoun and Harriott

"The impunity with which these river pirates were allowed to plunder induced others to do the same; until their numbers, their outrage increased to so great a height as to threaten to overthrow the commerce of the Port of London." (John Harriott)

Colquhoun and Harriott were uniquely qualified and experienced, with complementary qualities, to curb river crime. Patrick Colquhoun was a successful Scottish businessman turned lawyer. John Harriott, who had been in turn both a naval and an army officer, was, unlike his shrewd, judicial partner, a blunt and impetuous man. They both wanted to quell – by lawful force if necessary – the anarchy which they foresaw could destroy the nation; they were also, however, ardent reformers who recognised that flawed social systems were responsible for much of the existing crime.

Both men were of the same age. Harriott was an adventurer who, after a little schooling at Great Stambridge in Essex, saw action as a Royal Navy midshipman, survived a shipwreck, and rose to the rank of Post Captain before he was 21. Colquhoun was educated at Dumbarton Grammar School. Orphaned at the age of fifteen, he emigrated to America, settled in Virginia and so prospered there that when he was 21, in 1765, he was able to return to Britain and establish himself as a Glasgow merchant.

Harriott transferred to the Merchant Service, roaming the world from the Baltic to the Indies, and in 1766 he spent several months with American Indians. In 1768, still in his early twenties, he joined the East India Company's private militia, leading sepoy (native Indian) battalions in battle, doing duty as a deputy judge advocate and even acting for a time as chaplain. A nasty musket wound in the leg ended his soldiering; so, after lengthy visits to Sumatra and the Cape, he too eventually came home.

Colquhoun, meantime, had been busy proving himself a loyal British subject. During the American War of Independence he was one of twelve principal contributors to raise a Glasgow regiment that later became the 83rd of the Line. He undertook a fact-finding visit to Manchester in 1788 to acquaint the Prime Minister, William Pitt (the Younger) with conditions in the British cotton trade, and the following year he went to Flanders and the old Brabant province of Belgium to advertise the merits of Lanarkshire and other British muslins. He also promoted local trade and commerce and in 1782 was elected Lord Provost

4. Patrick Colquhoun   *5. John Harriott*

of Glasgow. Re-elected the following year, he established Glasgow's Chamber of Commerce and served as its first Chairman. He was nominated 'Father of the City of Glasgow' and was made a Justice of the Peace.

Back in England, Harriott had a short spell as an underwriter in the wine trade, then married for the first time and settled in his native Essex. There in 1781-2 he reclaimed from the Thames the island of Rushley, located between Great Wakering and Foulness. This entailed draining 200 acres of land, submerged at spring tides by several feet of water, and enclosing them with three miles of embankment, after which he built farm buildings upon the land and sank wells. For this the Society of Arts awarded him its Gold Medal. He also became Surveyor of the Essex Roads and a local magistrate. But he also endured some cruel setbacks. Fire in 1790 destroyed his home and all but one of his farm buildings, which he restored to house his family. Then, just as his reclaimed land was beginning to yield crops, an abnormally high tide burst through the embankment and flooded it with salt water. He was ruined, although sympathetic creditors spared him from bankruptcy. In 1791 (then 46 years old and twice widowed) he emigrated with his third wife and three children to America, where four years' travelling did little to recoup their fortunes.

A couple of years earlier Colquhoun had moved to London, probably hoping with his American experience to be given a government trade appointment but, as a result of the War of Independence, the former trans-Atlantic colonies were lost forever. Instead he became a stipendiary (paid) magistrate, under the Police Act 1792, sitting at Worship Street in Finsbury. Later he transferred to the Bench of Queen Square, Westminster, where, except for a notable two years leave of absence devoted to establishing the Thames Court, he would remain until he retired at the age of 71. Living in Wapping he saw how local people preyed upon the river and must also have been aware of the earlier magisterial work done at Bow Street by the Fielding half-brothers, Henry (1748-52) and Sir John who followed him. Colquhoun published anonymously in 1795 '*A TREATISE on the Police of the Metropolis...Explaining the Various Crimes and Misdemeanours which at PresentFelt As a Press Upon the Community; and Suggesting Remedie for their Prevention...to the Institution of a RIVER POLICE for securing Commercial Property, in the Port of London, against unexampled Depredations which have been heretofore experienced, and improving the Morals of the Maritime Labourers.*'

It was widely read. *The Times* newspaper reviewed it favourably, government ministers quoted from it and the King himself expressed interest. The writer's identity soon became known and, in 1797, the University of Glasgow conferred upon him the Degree of LL.D. So he became Doctor Colquhoun.

By then Harriott had come back to England yet again – his fourteenth Atlantic crossing. He was later to lose his beloved only daughter Sarah, shipwrecked in a dreadful Indian Ocean tornado, on her way home to England with her wounded husband, an army major. One of his sons would be killed while commanding a gun-brig attacking and taking Batavia; the other, who had followed his father into the army of the East India Company, lost a leg to a cannon ball at the Battle of Delhi. Harriott was more than once downcast but he struggled on, setting up a small factory to produce a ship's pump he had patented and which had been adopted by the Navy. His involvement with this company would later cause him to be falsely arraigned on criminal charges. He had a hand in the invention and patenting of several other mechanical devices: an engine for raising weights and working mills; an improved method of making and operating windlasses; and a fire escape.

At Queen Square, Colquhoun strove for reform with a proposal, ahead of its time, for an open prison; he helped establish a Quaker soup kitchen; he even suggested a fund to redeem from pawnbrokers' shops the goods and tools of honest and hard-working families who had been compelled to pledge them for cash to survive the cruel weather of 1794.

John Harriott, whose patriotism, like Colquhoun's, was always practical, wrote to the Lord Mayor of London on 27 February 1797 proposing a coastal defence system to keep a constant lookout for the French at a time when England stood alone against France. He had sufficient money that year also to give £500 to a 'Loyalty Fund' appeal by the Prime Minister. Beginning to concern himself with river crime, Harriott drew up a plan to put afloat a dedicated body of well-paid and properly trained armed men in uniform, empowered to stop, search and detain suspects and goods. He presented this to the Lord Mayor, Brook-Watson, who was also Conservator of the River Thames, but His Worship said he could do nothing. Harriott contacted other interested parties, including the Elder Brethren of the Trinity Corporation, but without response. Eventually, on 30 December that year, he wrote to the Home Secretary, the Duke of Portland, enclosing his plan, but was again disappointed when there was no reaction, probably due to the cost of his proposal, which he had estimated at £14,000 a year. Six months then elapsed which, unknown to him, were not uneventful.

Colquhoun had meanwhile submitted his own plan for guarding the port to the West India Company of Merchants & Planters. This was astute for the annual loss from pilfering endured by the Company was about £25,000, ten times higher than that of the more powerful East India Company which had better facilities for handling and storing their cargoes. The East India Company had its own dock at Rotherhithe, its own covered lighters, spacious and well-maintained warehouses, specially appointed Revenue officers and an advantageous arrangement whereby duty was not paid until after the sale of goods.

The merchandise of the West India Merchants & Planters, on the other hand, was transported in open lighters and hoys owned by private contractors. These often lay a long time at moorings or berths where they might sink or be looted. Their cargoes were also dumped on quays and in warehouses with indifferent security; and West Indian sugar, coffee and rum were easier for thieves to dispose of than silk, carpets and porcelain from the East Indies. At meetings in January and February 1798 the West India Company voted to adopt Colquhoun's plan and forwarded it to the Duke of Portland for approval. The Government agreed to back the scheme provided the company paid for it.

John Harriott had a cousin – John Staples, a magistrate at the Shadwell Police Office – and, through him, Harriott received an unexpected invitation to dine with Patrick Colquhoun on 22 April 1798. Both men were by then 53 years old. Colquhoun was impressed by this versatile and resourceful master mariner, soldier, farmer, writer (and poet), inventor, engineer, magistrate and public servant. Harriott, in his turn, acknowledged Colquhoun's ability to get things done. He left his own operational plan with the Doctor, who generously promised to pass it on to Secretary of State, Henry Dundas and did so.

The pace of events accelerated. On 16 May following, Lord Penrhyn, Chairman of the West India Merchants & Planters, showed Colquhoun and Harriott a letter from the Duke of Portland confirming government backing for their proposals which were now costed at only £5,000 a year. The Chancellor agreed to find £980, leaving the West India Company to pay the rest. With some central funding assured, the West India Merchants resolved to put the plan to work at once and on 11 June the Duke of Portland wrote to Colquhoun asking him to become Superintending Magistrate of the Marine Police – a substitute would be found for his duties at Queen Square until further notice. Henry Dundas directed the Merchants to lease premises at or near Wapping New Stairs and on 15 June they reported the acquisition of No. 259. They also recommended to the Secretary of State that John Harriott should be the Resident Magistrate and so his name was added to the list of Justices for the Counties of Middlesex, Surrey and Kent. Colquhoun and Harriott's task was no less than to tame the Port of London; but, in their hearts, the two men also hoped to reform the malefactors.

CHAPTER THREE

Chaos

"...a Police must be resorted to upon the broad scale of General Prevention –
Mild in its operation – Effective in its results; having justice and humanity for
its basis..."   (Patrick Colquhoun)

The Port of London was chaotic. Over 1,700 ships might be there at once but no system existed to accommodate them. A master tied up or dropped anchor where he could; square-rigged barques tangled with fore-and-aft schooners; smacks and sloops squeezed between Dutch galliots, hatch boats and hoys; fishing luggers lay alongside pilot boats. The skyline was spindled with masts, and idle spars, their rigging and scandalized sails limply drying. Massive East India merchantmen, 1,000 tons laden and drawing up to 24 feet, could navigate no further than Blackwall where the silted, undredged channel stopped them, and the river was so crowded that it might take four days for these ships to work their way even that far (forty miles inland) from the sea. Smaller vessels were able to penetrate a further four miles upriver to the medieval London Bridge. Three-hundred-ton Baltic timber ships, surrounded by rafts of unloaded logs awaiting removal, each took up the space of a dozen ships and over 400 of them came to London each year. Add to all that the to-and-fro of small boats, and more than 8,000 craft might be crowded into the Pool of London, a term which came to mean that stretch of water from two miles above London Bridge, downstream for six miles to Cuckold's Point. At times a waterman could hardly find a way to row across, yet thieves might roam unhindered on foot from one vessel to another. Bumboatmen, who sculled from ship to ship selling consumables (including liquor) to crews, had scope for all kinds of malpractice and were always suspect. There was a Bumboat Act of 1761:

'...to prevent the committing of Thefts and Frauds by persons
navigating Bumboats and other boats upon the River Thames.'

Under this Act such boats plying between London Bridge and Hope Point had to be registered, marked, numbered and licensed by the Trinity Corporation. Seven or more owners or masters could authorise the search and detention of boats with goods stolen or suspected stolen from ships on the river and take the boatmen before a Justice, when convicted offenders might be transported for seven (receivers for fourteen) years. It deterred nobody. Fourteen years went by before the Act was even implemented, when the average fine was just forty shillings. The bumboatmen formed a savings club so that, if caught (which was seldom), the accumulated subscriptions to this thieves' league paid their fines.

There were only twenty quays where dutiable goods could legally be landed or loaded, and stacked to be examined and weighed by Customs officers, before going into large warehouses or aboard ships. The Crown had established this legal quay system over 200 years earlier, in the first year of Elizabeth I's reign. They were all located on the north shore above Tower Ditch and below London Bridge, a quayside frontage, that had not increased since Tudor times, of just 1,419 feet for 545 ships. Four of these quays were owned by the Customs and the mighty East India Company. The rest belonged to – or were leased by – other companies and individual wharfingers, some of whom understandably allowed goods to be landed only when they were also to be stored in their warehouses. Most of the quays were unsuited to cope with the large and valuable cargoes which overflowed from their inadequate storage facilities.

Men hung around wharves and quays, offering to work by the hour or day as porters. During busy spells they quietly pilfered, concealing stuff beneath their long dock workers' aprons; when work went slack, a few would stage a scuffle, enabling others under cover of the distraction to secure pickings they could all later share.

Within the warehouses, goods were no more secure. Samples of sugar had to be taken from casks to grade it, officially one and a half pounds weight from each hogshead, but the coopers generally took five pounds for themselves and left as much again on top of the cask for the warehousemen. The sugar in casks made lighter than they should have been was dampened to make up the missing weight. Sweepers put the loose sugar into a spare cask hidden in some dark corner which, when full, was sold to a receiver and another empty one put in its place. Sometimes two were on the go at once. Such losses, averaging 16 pounds from each one of 130,000 hogsheads, cost owners £70,000 a year.

Rum too was prized, much of it ending up in receivers' shops and pubs. Out of a fleet of 370-400 ships, one in every four or five would be visited by coopers with their jiggers, skins and bladders; ashore, excessive samples were syphoned off in the warehouses.

Only the smallest ships could be poked into the shallow riverside berths where the water at the various wharves, stairs, docks and holes was often no more than one foot deep, although the average depth mid-channel from Blackwall to London Bridge was 16 feet. Coming and going was consequently restricted to about two hours either side of high water. Then, as the tide receded, the 'mudlarks' arrived. These were the weakest and poorest of river parasites, mostly women, children and old men. Barefoot they grubbed over the stinking foreshore – risking broken glass and infection – for anything that might bring the price of their next meal and bed: old rope; iron; bones; tools; small pieces of coal; chips of wood; and other jetsam. They even waded out waist-deep with baskets, kettles, caps and such-like to hold their finds. It was that or starve, yet pickings must have been meagre for nearly 300 of them worked the north shore, at fourteen sets of stairs and slipways from Execution Dock downstream to lower Limehouse Hole. Up to fifty gathered at the most central location, King James Stairs, Wapping Wall. Some lingered near dock gates to catch copper nails and other ship repair materials dropped down to them, to be reclaimed later (for a small reward) by the labourers.

To cope with increased traffic, permission was granted between 1793-9 for the British coasting trade and certain eastern countries to land goods of lesser dutiable value at 23 'sufferance' wharves. Only five of these were on the north side of the river. The other eighteen were across the water at Rotherhithe, with its mingled stinks from distilleries, tanneries, slaughterhouses and ropewalks. This augmented the working frontage, bringing the number of quayside berths up to 879, a total of 3,676 feet – but it was still not enough; and, as many of these wharves were remote, in an area noted mainly for its brothels, bear-baiting, hogs and fogs, it increased cargo-handling and theft.

The legal quays and sufferance wharves between them operated an exclusive trading monopoly, so the vast majority of ships had no alternative but to discharge and load midstream using barges or lighters. A lighter was a 'dumb' barge (lacking mast and sails or, later, an engine) which had to be driven with the tide by a man wielding a 25-foot long sweep oar. It had a capacious 100-ton hold and was called a lighter because discharging into it 'lightened' cargo vessels. Unloading with lighters took from two to six weeks. There were not enough of them; without tugs, their movements were dictated by the tides; they couldn't work in rough water or bad weather; and, once laden, they had to queue for a turn at the quaysides. Over 3,000 barges and lighters were engaged in this shuttle service. Another 2,000 transported goods up and down the Thames and inland along its tributaries and by canal to the Midlands and the west country. This piecemeal movement of goods meant there was always £5 million worth lying around on land or water, exposed to deterioration and depredation.

Watermen and lightermen claimed the right to keep for themselves the inevitable drippings and spillages in their craft from imperfectly packed wet and dry goods, but cases and casks were deliberately dropped and damaged, secretly broached or blatantly broken open. When one West India merchant, irked by the amount he was losing, paid a surprise visit to a barge full with barrels of his oil, he found them stowed with the bungs downwards, each one loosened. Nearly half the contents had drained into the barge's hold and, if he had left it a day longer, all this oil would have been claimed by the lighterman.

What could not be had by stealth was openly snatched by river pirates. About 100 ruffians in gangs armed with cutlasses and pistols were active between St Katharine's Dock and Gravesend. Having picked out a likely ship in daylight, they would board it at night, overpowering anyone who stood in their way. Entire deck cargoes were carried off. Bulky cordage (such as running rigging) and large ironwork was taken; boats' gear, clothing, stores and provisions, to the value of £45,000 each year, were grabbed. Laden barges and lighters were simply cut adrift and taken to hideaways where they could be looted at leisure. Far from the Caribbean or Spanish Main of later Hollywood films, much of this piracy occurred within sight of St Paul's Cathedral. The master of an American ship lying at East Lane Tier, just a mile downstream from London Bridge, up at dawn on a summer morning heard voices forward. Looking over the bow he saw men in a boat alongside and demanded to know what they were doing. One of them looked up at him. "Ah, Captain, is that you?" he said. The master repeated his question. Drily the man replied; "Only weighed your anchor, Captain, and cut your cable. That's all. Good morning, Captain." And away they went, with his costly mooring tackle, up with the tide through the bridge. Pursuit was impossible. Anyway, no local would have dared try to stop them.

Thieving and piracy decreased only when the Press Gangs dragged river workers off to man British warships. The Royal Navy had always looked to the Thames as a prime source of manpower; indeed the Waterman's Company gained some relief from forcible recruitment by voluntarily supplying 500-2,000 men at a time for naval service; but not until 1859, long after the Battle of Trafalgar, were Thames watermen freed from the hazard of impressment. This was not all bad. When in peacetime they returned, so did crime. It had to be stopped.

CHAPTER FOUR

Action

"We seized the bull by the horns, and never quitted our hold for upwards
of two years... and we succeeded, by our joint efforts, in bringing into reasonable
order some thousands of men, who had long considered plunder as a privilege..."
(John Harriott)

On the afternoon of the first day John Harriott led a sortie of freshly-sworn
Marine Police constables to intercept a gang of coal heavers coming ashore,
within sight of the Wapping Police Office, in a boat almost sinking under the
weight of stolen sacks of coal. Free coal, they asserted when stopped, was their
right. He gave them one alternative to prosecution – put it back; they refused
and resisted arrest but were overpowered.

About 1,400 Wapping stevedores – mostly Irish – earned a living manhandling
coal, in sacks and baskets, from ship to barge or quayside. It was filthy work
needing brute strength but there was plenty of it. To fuel London's steam-driven
machinery, and to satisfy a growing domestic demand from the one million
people now living in the capital city, more than half of British coasters were
colliers which sailed in fleets from the burgeoning north-east mining industry.
Bulky-hulled craft, unable to beat into contrary winds, they were often delayed
by adverse weather. Then, with conditions favourable, ninety colliers would
arrive all at once to unload their cargoes of sea coal and glut the market. The
sweating coal heavers, labouring in a cloud of black dust that hung in the air,
appeared half-savage to the city folk who saw them in action. Masters of colliers,
competing for this labour, offered the men free coal; but the coal heavers took
more than they could ever burn themselves – £20,000 worth each year – and
sold it in an illegal public market at the end of Blackmore Alley, in the parish
of St John, close by Execution Dock.

Harriott brought his prisoners in front of Patrick Colquhoun, who patiently
explained the law, warned them of the penalties, and then discharged them
with a caution. He and Harriott both knew that no locals had ever bought coal
– even the barefoot children picked it up from the foreshore or took it from
barges and carried it home. They grew up knowing no better. Over 2,000 barges
were needed to off-load the collier fleet when it was in port. Another 1,000
were left moored and laden midstream or berthed alongside as storage vessels
for merchants to draw supplies from, when needed, but they were a source of
free coal for anyone with a bucket or sack and no conscience.

6. The Thames Police headquarters at Wapping; etching by James McNeil Whistler in 1859.

Colquhoun also understood how a coal heaver could be compelled to steal. Although his earnings were comparatively high, perhaps eight shillings a day (two or three times a Police waterman's pay), he took home much less. Eight hundred of them were controlled by twenty or so local publicans who for a start, demanded 25% commission from each man for every ship discharged. Any man unemployed was advanced five shillings a day to keep him in gin and porter but these could only be had from the publican who loaned him the money (and had to be repaid later from earnings). Then again, liquor to the value of twelve shillings was sent out to ships being worked, whether or not the men asked for it; and, if they refused it, liquor money was stopped from their wages and they were not hired again. So they were always in debt to the leech-like publicans. Such desperate men had to be reformed, yet at first they failed to appreciate judicial leniency and resented Police interference. Three months later men on both sides would be killed in a ferocious confrontation.

Colquhoun and Harriott's plan was for five Surveyors to patrol the river in shifts, day and night, rowed in open galleys by dependable watermen. Another four Surveyors were to visit ships being loaded and unloaded, where Ship Constables would supervise the gangs of lumpers. A Surveyor of Quays, with two Assistants, had thirty Police Quay Guards to safeguard cargoes on shore. The two magistrates would try offenders brought before them for misdemeanours and commit indictable offences for trial by judge and jury. Surveyors and Constables were authorised to stop, search and detain suspects, to bring them before the magistrates at the Police Office. Anyone convicted of obstructing them in their duty could be transported overseas for seven years.

The scheme began on 2 July 1798 with 215 men including six Boat Surveyors. The magistrates personally instructed them in their duties. Surveyors, Land Officers, Ship Constables and Quay Guards took an oath to God and King, while watermen and lumpers simply swore to be faithful to the trust reposed in them. Vigilance, zeal, firmness and discretion were required of all the men. Truncheons, cutlasses and firearms were to be used only in self defence, as a last resort, and never to threaten people. They were closely supervised and strictly disciplined. Taking bribes, drunkenness, absence from post, or other lapses from the highest standards – which happened, even with chosen men – resulted in summary dismissal, in disgrace (and that meant without pay). Surveyors were paid £75-100 a year, putting them in the lower middle class. A waterman's top wage was 23 shillings a week, enabling him with care to keep himself and his family out of debt, on top of which, to encourage diligence, they would also receive one tenth the value of all seizures made.

The Marine Police Office was sub-divided into four established sections, all under the direct control of Colquhoun and Harriott:

1.   Judicial Department

1	Superintending Magistrate: Patrick Colquhoun (unpaid)
1	Resident Magistrate: John Harriott
	Judicial Clerks
	Chief Constable
7	Petty Constables

Sub-total 11 (£980)

2.   Marine Police (or Preventive) Department

1	Chief Clerk & Cashier
1	House Surveyor & Superintendent of Ship Constables
4	Boat Surveyors, visiting ships, etc.
5	Perambulating Surveyors, for river duty
18	Watermen
1	Surveyor of the Quays
2	Assistant Surveyors
30	Quay Guards

Sub-total 62 (£2,650)

3.   Discharge Department
employing registered lumpers to discharge ships*

1	Superintendent of Lumpers
1	Collecting Clerk
1	Assistant Clerk

Sub-total 3 (£270)

4. General Department for the Accounts
1   Cashier
1   Collecting Clerk
1   Housekeeper & Office Keeper
1   House Watchman
     (also 1 Solicitor)
     Sub-total 4 (£200)

PLUS cost of house, taxes, law charges, stationery, coal, candles,
boat expenses and premiums for services.
     Sub-total £900

GRAND TOTAL £5,000

It was not part of Colquhoun and Harriott's original plan for the Marine Police
to find labourers to unload West India ships; but a registration scheme for
lumpers used to handling West India cargoes was pressed upon them and
adopted. This extra manpower amounted to 80 master lumpers and, as needed,
about 900 working lumpers (who were required to wear special uniforms in
which goods could not be concealed), also 220 Ship Constables (all paid for by
ships' owners using their services). So the Marine Police ended up with effective
control of more than 1,000 full-time and casual workers. So they began – but
would it work?

7. A Thames Police patrol at night.

CHAPTER FIVE

Impact

"It is the dread of the existing power of immediate detection, and the certainty of punishment as the consequence of this detection, that restrains men of loose morals from the commission of offences." (Patrick Colquhoun)

The plan was put into effect a bit at a time. Initial advertisements sought 35 foremen (with some knowledge of seamanship), seventy constables and 350 lumpers. Constables and foremen were paid five shillings a day; lumpers got three shillings and sixpence. These men were divided into 35 gangs, each consisting of two constables, one foreman and ten lumpers, the gangs to be changed around every Monday to lessen any chance of collusion and corruption.

Because Ship Constables were paid by the shippers requesting their services – not from Police funds – they were self-financing from the outset. When owners asked for them, two Ship Constables were posted to a vessel, where their first duty was to nail to the mast a notice:

CAUTION AGAINST PILLAGE AND PLUNDER
Marine Police Establishment,
259 Wapping New Stairs,
under the sanction of Government, and at the earnest desire of the
MERCHANTS and SHIP-OWNERS

A CAUTION

For the express purpose of rescuing the Port of London from the great injury and disgrace which has arisen from the enormous Pillage and Plunder which has heretofore prevailed on board West-India and other Ships, and in Lighters conveying Cargoes on shore, as well as upon Legal Quays where Goods are landed, a Marine Police-Office has been established, to which are attached above Six Hundred Lumpers for working out Ships, and also Two Hundred Constables, armed with the authority of the Law to act as Guards and Watchmen on board each Ship under discharge, together with a proper number of Boats commanded by Police Surveyors and navigated by Officers of Justice, with power to search, seize, and apprehend all persons whatsoever suspected of taking, or having in their possession, Sugar,

Rum, Coffee, Cotton, Ginger, Pimento, Indigo, or any article what-soever, composing the Cargo, Stores, or Materials, of any Ship or Vessel in the River Thames, and to bring all offenders to Justice without respect of persons.

It is therefore hoped that this early caution will prevent every description of persons either working or acting in any capacity on boat or Ships under discharge – and all persons whatsoever – from making free even with the smallest quantity of Sugar or other articles, as, in case of detection, (which will be certain) nothing can prevent the ignominy of a Prosecution for Felony, and the ultimate punishment in case of conviction.

The wordy warning remained in place throughout discharging and loading and was read aloud each morning by one of the officers so that those unable to read could not later plead ignorance of it. Every lumper and cooper who came aboard or went ashore was searched for tools and stolen goods and their work closely watched, with one P.C. always in the hold and the other on deck. The latter had to be a good writer because he recorded all goods in transit and their destinations, accompanying lighters to the shore and handing their contents over to the Quay Guards who signed for them. Thus cargoes were protected at every stage from arrival to final delivery or departure.

Ship Constables were instructed to treat Customs & Excise officers with respect but not to let them take over any part of Police duties. Watermen's boats were not to idle near ships without a good reason, and from sunset to dawn a lighted lantern was hung in the main shrouds, with another at the gangway, to show Surveyors where Constables were posted and to discourage thieves. It certainly deterred those it was aimed at. Colquhoun reported;

> "...a gang of Lumpers, after coming on board to discharge a West India ship, quitted their employment instantly on the appearance of the Police Officers, and on their reading the Caution... they went on board for Plunder, under an impression that the Ship was not under the Police; finding themselves disappointed, they resorted to an unguarded ship."

The service was established for West India ships but Colquhoun offered it to other owners, who could apply to the Superintendent of Lumpers at the Marine Police Office, when master lumpers or foremen would be recommended and two Ship Constables assigned to each vessel. They were entitled to free daily and nightly inspections by the patrolling Surveyors and a careful record of each undertaking was kept. To encourage ship owners and masters to take advantage of the new system, charges were the lowest in the Port; two shillings a ton had to be paid in advance to the Lumping Department, plus an extra 5% to defray the cost of engaging a lumping gang, but any surplus was returned to the ship on completion of her discharge. The Marine Police made no profit.

Harriott's hand-picked Surveyors, who were mostly waterwise ex-shipmasters, had to share his enthusiasm and commitment. Daily they faced ruffians and rogues who, like their fathers and grandfathers, had previously done what they wanted and to whom plunder was a perk. Six hours on, twelve off, as one boat's crew came in every two hours, another went out on patrol. It was a tiring routine. As well as the day and night visits to ships under the Institution's protection, and attention to all other West India ships, a Surveyor's duties included: checking that all sugar barges had secure tarpaulins; looking out for signs of fire (accidental or malicious), a major fear when ships consisted of wood, rope, canvas and tar; and telling the Magistrates of any shipmaster above Blackwall receiving gunpowder on board. The Magistrates required Surveyors to keep diaries of all occurrences and to report them each morning. They also had to compile detailed quarterly reports of services performed, work achieved and the general state of river security, to be submitted the day each officer received his salary (no doubt as a spur to vigilance).

During the night of 22 October 1798 the brig *Tyger* was found adrift on the tide and re-secured by two Police boat crews. Then, at 3 am on 20 January 1799, an American ship – the *Amiable* – broke loose in a severe snow storm and bore down upon an adjacent tier of shipping. If the vessel had collided with it, the momentum would have carried all away. Mayhem was averted by a Surveyor and his crew who (dutifully still out and about in the appalling conditions) boarded the errant ship and, helped by the mate, steered clear and then re-moored it.

By such actions Colquhoun and Harriott's officers began a concept and tradition adopted later by the Metropolitan Police – and all its imitators – that public acceptance of a deterrent Police role is only possible when they are also seen to be friends and rescuers by anyone in trouble.

A Surveyor overtook a couple of men in a boat at midnight and seized two trunks of expensive printed muslin. Before the examining magistrate, it transpired, one of the culprits had signed on aboard the ship merely to get at the cargo while it was being stowed. Stealing to order for a receiver who had already agreed to buy the goods, he took the two trunks and locked them away elsewhere on the vessel. The snag was that the key he would later need to recover the goods was itself locked up at night. So, during the day (before it could be missed) he took it ashore, had it copied and restored the original by early afternoon to its proper place. A little before midnight the two thieves rowed out to the ship, used the duplicate key to retrieve the goods and put them into their boat.

In this way a lot of home produced exports, on which Excise duty had been paid, never even left the London river and the fabric in this case would have disappeared but for the presence and alertness of Harriott's river patrol. One of the prisoners confessed and asked for other such thefts to be taken into consideration. Colquhoun particularly disliked this kind of crime, as losses often went undiscovered until a ship arrived in a foreign port, when the captain would be held accountable for the shortage. He knew of at least one instance when an unfortunate master had been accused of larceny and dismissed in disgrace, only for the real thieves to be apprehended later.

The impact of the river patrols was beyond doubt. After just five days *TheTimes* reported:

> 'The new establishment of the Marine Police Office at Wapping promises to afford the greatest protection to the mercantile interest. No branch of the police has been more neglected, arising from its not being well understood; and no magistrate could undertake the superintendence with so much propsect of utility as Mr. Colquhoun.
>
> The object of the institution is to destroy one of the greatest systems of depredation that ever existed in any country, besides the immense collateral advantages which will arise to the revenue in the check given to illicit trade; and also to the metropolis and country at large, in the security which will be extended to the shipping against incendiaries, by means of river-guards, which will be attached to this office, and which will ply up and down in the night.'

Within a few months watermen gave up loitering near ships being unloaded; low water saw no mudlarks; scuffle-hunters and long apron men abandoned the quaysides; light horsemen, pirates and plunderers disappeared from the night. Some retreated downstream to the lower reaches, for the time being beyond the oars of the Marine Police patrols. The Port, which previously teemed with dubious characters when West India fleets discharged, went quiet. There was a lull, but the rule of law was not yet established and it was the coal heavers who chose to go down fighting.

CHAPTER SIX

Riot

"I immediately saw the necessity for prompt and resolute measures, for the infuriated madness of the assailants grew stronger every instant. Ordering the firearms, seeing to their loading, and giving necessary directions, seemed to electrify me and make me young again." (John Harriott)

It was a Tuesday evening, 16 October 1798, and the Magistrates were trying two coal heavers and a waterman's boy charged – yet again – with stealing coal. Each was found guilty and fined 40 shillings as an alternative to prison. Shortly afterwards, at about 8.30 pm, the narrow street outside the Police Office filled with the men's cronies backed by a mob hundreds strong. Most were armed with heavy sticks or cudgels. At least one, as it turned out, had a gun.

They were not only angry that habitual pilfering was under threat, but in common with many Londoners, they saw the establishment of an official police force as an attack on their civil liberty. The Marine Police was a radical innovation – there had been nothing like it before. Afloat or ashore, the sort of preventive policing by public consent which we know today was absent and, by many, unwanted. The 1792 Act under which Colquhoun was appointed to Queen Square merely set up seven Police Offices, each in the charge of a Magistrate with six Constables. Like the thief-taking Bow Street Runners – who were simply bounty hunters – these officers of the law only arrived on the scene *after* crimes had been committed and so were not true peace-keepers. Indeed the establishment of a regular Police was actively resisted, often by influential people. The Westminster Police Bill of 1785, brought by Sir Archibald Macdonald, Solicitor General of Pitt's government, was withdrawn due to strong opposition from the City of London; while the Whigs, under their leader Charles James Fox, believed the Tories would use such a force to repress the common people. The Bill was not reintroduced. So it was a new experiment that Colquhoun and Harriott had undertaken, to deter casual riverside lawbreakers by the certainty of detection, trial and conviction, converting the hardened remainder by means of firm but humane sentencing.

The mob besieged the building, yelling for the release of all the defendants. Some tried to force the street door but, locked and bolted on the inside, it proved too strong for them. There were only six or seven officers within the building, plus three City gentlemen who were witnesses at the Court hearings. One of this trio hid in the top of the house, the other two escaped by boat. The magistrates and their men might have got out too but they stayed.

The rioters prised up cobble stones from the carriageway and showered them at the shuttered and barred windows. Next they lifted and hurled 20-pound paving slabs, which smashed through, narrowly missing the men inside. Then they tried to shove brands of flaming wood through the breached shutters. If the attackers got into the building, or forced its occupants out by fire and smoke, Harriott was convinced, he and his colleagues would probably all be killed. He may have been the only person in the place who (thirty years earlier) had ever smelt gunpowder burnt in action, and it was he who commanded firearms to be made ready for use. As soon as the pistols were loaded, he gave the order to fire down into their attackers. One of the ring-leaders fell dead. The rioters retreated a short distance to Dung Wharf, dragging the body with them, swearing reprisals.

Both magistrates now showed their mettle. Patrick Colquhoun had the front door opened and, backed by their loyal handful of officers, Harriott and he went out onto the steps. There Colquhoun read aloud his copy of the Riot Act of 1715, which all magistrates were required to have to hand, calling upon the crowd to disperse or face arrest and punishment – which could be death. The lawful and time-honoured practice in riots (to which the English working class had been partial for centuries) was to allow an hour to elapse after any such reading before further action, but in this case the mob re-grouped and surged forward again. One officer close to Harriott and Colquhoun was shot through the palm of his hand by a pistol ball. Then one of their master lumpers, a stevedore named Gabriel Franks, collapsed crying out that he too had been shot. Harriott, blood up and careless of legal precedent, led his few men forward. Amazingly they won. Firing a few more pistol shots, police (outnumbered twenty to one) drove off the mob.

Franks was fatally wounded and died on the way to hospital. His name begins the Roll of Honour bearing those of thirty Thames Police officers killed on duty or active military service in the Division's 200-year history. Four rioters also died and several were wounded, although their exact casualties were never known for sure.

A breathing space had been gained but Harriott was preparing for a renewed attack when unexpected reinforcements arrived, members of the Wapping & Union Volunteer Corps, a sort of armed neighbourhood watch. At about 11 pm, hearing that the rioters were in a distant public house, the indomitable Harriott went off with the Volunteers, intent on arresting as many as he could find, but they were gone. The Volunteers patrolled the streets throughout the night and all remained quiet.

The Times next day reported the riot and told its readers of the Royal Pardon offered to anyone (except the killer of Gabriel Franks) who informed upon other rioters. There was £20 for information leading to the conviction of Franks' murderer but that person was never traced. Perhaps one or more of the notorious coal undertakers, their activities curtailed by the Marine Police, incited the coal heavers to violence. However it started, the steadfast Colquhoun and Harriott's victory was a turning point; if they had fled or failed, the establishment of a preventive, peace-keeping Police Force might have been delayed for at least another generation.

A week after the riot, on 23 October, the *London Gazette* announced that six coal heavers, with others, had been charged in connection with the disorder, and they were subsequently tried and convicted. One was hanged; the others transported overseas. Such sentencing was not unduly harsh for the time, since all convicted of rioting could be put to death. Colquhoun and Harriott, however, clearly believed their contemporary Jeremy Bentham's view that all punishment is in itself evil; for, although they had identified many more of the rioters, they agreed not to proceed against them. When these men appeared before them from time to time in court on other matters, they were reminded of their past behaviour and the consideration that had then been shown to them. Years later Harriott wrote that some of them could be seen keeping themselves and their families in honest comfort. In fact most of those who had once been enemies of the Marine Police in time reformed and became their allies.

CHAPTER SEVEN

Rule of Law

"...Police, conducted and enforced with purity, activity, vigilance and discretion."
(Patrick Colquhoun)

Three weeks after Harriott and Colquhoun had been besieged *The Times* printed:

> 'We are extremely glad to hear of the success of the new
> Marine Police Establishment in Wapping which offers so much
> accommodation as well as security to the merchants. It is
> astonishing the effect the institution has already had, in prevent-
> ing piracies and robberies, as well as illicit trade on the river...
> and the saving of the planters and merchants, and of course the
> revenue, in the protection afforded to the West India articles
> now under discharge, although it cannot be accurately ascer-
> tained, must amount to a very large sum.'

Despite assured savings and increased profits, many shippers – even some
in the West India fleet – did not at first take advantage of the protection offered.
Master lumpers and labour contractors who still controlled the Port's unreg-
istered labour force, clinging to their commissions and bribes, told shipmasters
and owners that Marine Police rates were more expensive. In fact they were
the cheapest. They also portrayed Police scrutiny as unacceptable State control.
A lot of junior Customs officers opposed the new system. Their basic wage
was as low as £10 a year, while a single bribe was commonly £50. Then again,
any officer unwilling to be bought might incur a savage beating. The Commissioner of Customs & Excise had, the previous year, requested military aid
because, he complained to the Treasury, organised gangs of smugglers did not
hesitate to murder any revenue man who tried to stop them.

Harriott's Surveyors had been instructed to treat Customs officers with
respect. It was a sensible policy but it must have been hard to obey in the early
days when so many contested the rule of law. Following a tip, the Marine Police
stopped some lumpers and coopers off a China ship. In the struggle that ensued,
so much tea was jettisoned that the surface of the river around them was turned
into a watery brew of the stuff. Only after quite a fight did the Police arrest
two of them. It turned out that as many as forty tea chests had been removed
from the ship, despite specially designed secure hatches, with the aid of junior

revenue officers. But even the Customs men must have seen sense after Police detected a boat carrying a lot of coffee ashore from a West India ship; the mate having attested in Court that that they had helped him with the theft, two revenue officers were convicted and hanged.

The Marine Police would have been disbanded had it not proved cost-effective but it was a highly profitable enterprise. The saving to the West India Company proprietors after a year was £150,000; the Crown also gained a very large sum in revenue; and this was achieved at a cost to the backers of less than £5,000, at least a thirty-fold return of their original outlay. Patrick Colquhoun's work throughout was, at his insistence, unpaid.

To overawe the lawbreakers Police activity at the outset was almost excessive. In the first twelve months there were 2,200 convictions for misdemeanours. As the eighteenth century turned into the nineteenth, nearly 200 persons were imprisoned. A further thirteen were committed for trial on indictment and some of these paid with their lives (were 'turned off' in the euphemistic yet clinical words of that time). For stealing one quarter of a pound (a tenth of a kilo) of cocoa, value four shillings, one luckless man was flogged the length of New Fresh Wharf, before having to endure a year of hard labour. Crime diminished. There were no felonies committed on ships under the Ship Constable scheme. Plunder of the more attractive commodities – sugar, coffee, tea, rum, ginger, etc. – fell to one-fifth of what it had been; theft from all West India produce was not one-fiftieth of previous years.

One private dockyard paid for a Constable to guard a West India ship while the outside of her hull below the waterline was sheathed with copper, an anti-fouling measure which would also combat tropical marine boring organisms. 1,600 copper sheets and ten bags of nails were ordered, the amount used previously on the same ship. When the job was done there were 113 sheets of copper and three bags of nails left over, presumably stolen before, a saving of £71 4s. 4d.

Not only did the rowing patrols of the Surveyors reduce crime but also the efficiency of the lumping and discharge department speeded up unloading, avoided costly delays, ended confusion at quaysides and unclogged river traffic. Many letters of appreciation for the work of the Marine Police were received by Colquhoun and Harriott. One signed by 30 shipmasters read:

> 'We, the undersigned Masters of Hamburgh Ships and
> Vessels, trading to the Port of London, being truly sensible of
> the manifest difference as to the security of Property, on the
> River Thames, arising from the vigilance of the Guard Boats
> and Officers of the Marine Police Institution, patrolling the river,
> by day and by night, do consider it our duty voluntarily and
> publicly to declare, that whereas, formerly our Cables, Hawsers,
> and every article of Ships' Stores, as well as the inward and
> outward Cargoes of our Ships, while delivering or taking in,

were continually subject to the greatest Plunder, by a set of
lawless banditti, that then infested the River:

    We have, since the establishment of the Marine Police Insti-
    tution, experienced the most beneficial effects, in the protection
    afforded by the Boats and Officers belonging to the Office; and
    in testimony do subscribe our names, and the name of the Ships
    and Vessels we respectively command."

Many similar letters were received from shippers, wharfingers, coal buyers
and factors, and (of course) the West India Merchants. These testimonials may
have been solicited by Colquhoun and Harriott, or their backers, all anxious
to show the venture's worth. Spontaneous or not, they are documentary evidence
of considerable satisfaction with the new Marine Police. At a General Meeting
of West-India Planters it was resolved that their Chairman, Lord Penrhyn;

    "...be requested to communicate the thanks of this Meeting to
    Mr. Colquhoun, for the zeal, ability, and perseverance with
    which he had endeavoured to form an effectual check to the
    system of Depredation, which prevailed on the River Thames."

And the Chairman added a personal note:

    "Lord Penrhyn feels a very particular satisfaction, in convey-
    ing the sentiments of the Meeting, and their approbration of Mr.
    Colquhoun's plan."

John Harriott seems to have been taken for granted. In giving credit for
execution of the scheme to Colquhoun alone His Lordship was not the only
one to overlook the role of the Resident Magistrate. The West India Merchants
made Colquhoun a gift from their funds of a piece of plate worth £500 and the
Russia Company gave him another piece worth 100 guineas. Of course the
diplomatic Dr Colquhoun was an ideal figurehead. Harriott, often curt and
impatient, made few friends. Although these two dissimilar men do not appear
to have clashed with one another, being overlooked by outsiders clearly vexed
Harriott. On 16 May 1799, Colquhoun had received a letter from H.M. Commissioner for the Navy asking how they could prevent theft of naval stores.
Marine Police sailing cutters were deployed and it soon stopped. Presumably
Colquhoun was thanked for this because Harriott peevishly wrote later:

    "In the organisation and carrying it into complete execution...
    I took a full share... I do not hesitate, then, to say, that the
    detection and prevention of these embezzlements and plunder-
    ing of government stores of all descriptions, have arisen almost
    exclusively from the vigilance of the Thames Police Officers
    under my own direction and superintendence."

Still it was Colquhoun whose advice was sought by many. The Secretary of the West India Merchants trading in London's competitor Port of Liverpool contacted him because they were enduring enormous losses, particularly of coffee destined for Manchester; and a Worcester proprietor of barges trading on the River Severn between Stourport and Bristol wondered how he might cut the loss of liquor, wine and £1,000 worth of salt a year.

It became obvious to many that the London scheme – and its funding – should be enlarged to cover all commerce within the Port. Colquhoun planned to present a Bill to Parliament which would consolidate the status of the Marine Police and make it permanent. He had the facts and figures. For the legal wording he went to a Queen Square neighbour, the English social and legal reformer Jeremy Bentham.

8. Senior Magistrate Ballantine, portrayed for the Illustrated London News, 14 November 1846, when he had served 25 years with the Thames Police Court.

CHAPTER EIGHT

Bentham's Bill

"...it surprises me to think that so much was achieved with so small a comparative strength, against the numerous strong hordes of desperately wicked men..."
(John Harriott)

Six months after the establishment of the Thames Police, Colquhoun began to outline a Bill to convert what was basically a private security body, albeit publicly subsidised, into a fully accountable statutory one. He asked Jeremy Bentham to draft the document. This should have reassured anyone still apprehensive about a Police Force, since it was Bentham who had written in his *Principles of Morals and Legislation*, published in 1789, that the object of all law should be the greatest happiness for the greatest number. Yet some opposed the Bill.

The City of London Corporation had enjoyed jurisdiction over the river, from London Bridge as far upstream as Staines, since Richard I sold them his river rights – but *not* his customs dues – in 1196 for £20,000 (£7 million at today's value) to raise money for the Crusades. Henry VII, Henry VIII, Elizabeth I and Queen Anne had all confirmed this Charter. The Lord Mayor was Bailiff and Conservator of the waters of the Thames and Medway, so Colquhoun wrote to him and pointed out that the Bill expressly excluded the City of London from Marine Police jurisdiction. Indeed, it not only preserved the City's ancient rights, it extended them. Despite these reassurances the Court of Common Council, on the advice of its lawyers, rejected the proposal on the ground that this new Thames Police would infringe the privileges of City merchants. The Corporation had done virtually nothing to fulfill their responsibility to regulate shipping, maintain wharves, stairs and landing places; still they were unable to accept the challenge of a River Police. They added weakly that it would interfere with the Corporation's plan – which had not been touched for over 50 years – for improvements.

Junior Customs officers, the Company of Watermen, and many of the Port's licensed porters, carters and carriers predictably joined forces against the Bill. The East India Company and the West India Merchants were all for it. So too were the Russian, Mediterranean, Turkish, Canadian and United States traders. In the course of several meetings held during 1799 they resolved to send a deputation to the Duke of Portland, stressing the importance of extending Police protection to all traders using the Port.

The Government hesitated, as any extra burden on the Treasury at this time was unwelcome. The economy had been hurt by the Napoleonic Wars, there had been a bad harvest, and the country was short of food and upkeep of the Army and Navy was draining away the Bank of England's reserves.   The population, too, was multiplying and would go from under four million in the sixteenth century to 25 million by 1850.

Pitt offered £2,000 a year (and would probably have upped that sum) to support the existing Force, rather than approach Parliament with a more comprehensive scheme which might incidentally spoil his own plan for a Metropolitan Police. When, as a compromise, it was suggested that the Thames Office should combine with a civil force at Shadwell, Bentham was outraged. He wrote a long letter to Lord Colchester expressing doubt of the advantages of combining the two offices and pointed out that it would be a great injustice to Colquhoun;

> "...His services have been gratuitous... he has fed the estab-
> lishment out of his own pocket...he has sitten at it to be shot at,
> and has been shot at, and seen a man put to death at his side...
> Is it consistent with generosity to discard him and... to put a set
> of strangers to reap the fruit of what he has sown?"

Lord Colchester was for the Bill and sympathetic but, out of favour with the Treasury, he could do little to help. Colquhoun had more success with Henry Dundas who promised to take charge of the Bill and bring it to the next Parliamentary session, where it was eventually passed (with amendments) for the limited period of seven years and became law on 28 July 1800.

Colquhoun had always intended to return to the Bench at Queen Square and soon afterwards he did so. Under the new arrangement, however, he became the first Receiver or fiscal administrator for the Thames Marine Police. All fines and fees would be paid to him monthly and he was to provide the Secretary of State with a quarterly account.

Court business would be conducted by Harriott, continuing as Resident Magistrate, with two other stipendiaries, each to be paid £400 a year. They were empowered to appoint and dismiss Constables (up to a specified maximum number) who could be employed on land as well as water, and also allowed up to thirty Surveyors. Annual expenditure was increased to £8,000. The Thames magistrates now had jurisdiction along the whole course of the river and in the adjacent counties of Middlesex, Surrey, Kent and Essex, with specific powers to control coffee houses where thieves, prostitutes and toughs gathered, planned robberies and hid loot. Greater preventive powers were given. They could stop, search and detain anyone suspected 'on reasonable grounds' of stealing property (under the old Bumboat Act offenders could be arrested only if 'found committing' crime). The Government decided that it was not part of Police duty to license lumpers, who would in future be controlled with byelaws. This had been an addition to Colquhoun's original plan for the West India company. Now it was dropped.

John Harriott was joined on the Bench by William Kinnaird and William Braggs. He never hid his opinion that all Thames magistrates should have maritime, as well as judicial, expertise and be able to quell an affray – in other words, they should be like him. Neither Kinnaird nor Braggs understood ships or sailors and they both lived some distance from the river. So when they were required to submit an operational plan for approval by the Secretary of State (because Bentham's Bill did not say exactly how the River Guards should be either led or supervised) it was arranged that Harriott would, in addition to his magisterial duties, be the Superintendent to deploy and direct the river officers. Harriott took on this extra load voluntarily but later wished that he had insisted upon payment. He put in many more hours of hard work than either of the other two Magistrates; also, as the arrangement was never ratified, he was from time to time reproved by the Secretary of State for acting on his own initiative and not consulting his colleagues. Not that he was ever in awe of rank or influence. When an elderly gentleman – obviously not up to the rigours of duty afloat in all weathers – applied for a boat officer's vacancy, producing a reference from the Secretary of State, Harriott flatly turned him down and told the Minister that he would not be responsible for efficient river policing if he had to appoint such men.

In most textbooks which recount the history of England's police, Colquhoun's name alone appears; little or no mention is ever made of John Harriott's unstinted efforts; yet Colquhoun was away from the Bench at Queen Square for just two years, whereas Harriott gave the rest of his life – nearly twenty years – to the Marine Police. It was his strict leadership, brooking no incompetence or indiscipline, that moulded the men to their roles both afloat and ashore. They even did pike and cutlass drill.

When the West India Docks were opened at Poplar on the Isle of Dogs in 1802, the Constables taken on to guard them were attached to the Thames Police Office. This practice continued with other later docks. The men obeyed the orders of the dock authorities, who paid them, but their first allegiance was to the Thames Magistrates. So crucial did the docks become to City financiers that, in 1805, the Bank of England installed a wind direction vane so that traders could estimate the time a cargo entering the London river might take to reach them. No wonder then, in 1807 (when the 1800 enabling Act was about to expire), even a cash-strapped Government could see that the Marine Police annual grant of £8,000 was value for money. Parliament accordingly extended the Act for a further seven years, but Harriott was soon to undergo another personal ordeal.

CHAPTER NINE

Trial

"...danger is immediate and at all times to be apprehended."
(Patrick Colquhoun)

In October 1808, the Chief Clerk to the Marine Police, a man named H. M. Tomlins, was unable to account for fees and fines amounting to £247 10s. 0d which had been paid to him. He failed to answer questions, stayed away from the Police Office for several days, and was then suspended from duty by the Magistrates. He eventually settled the account with Colquhoun and resigned. His successor Walter Gullifer lasted only six months. He too was suspended, for disobedience as well as misuse of public money. But, when Harriott interrogated him, he and Tomlins retaliated, alleging that Harriott – never a popular man – was the guilty one. He challenged them to put their allegation in writing and forced their hands with a report to the Secretary of State requesting an enquiry.

Three investigating magistrates were appointed. Harriott, expecting a quick decision in his favour, meanwhile took no action against the two Clerks and was flabbergasted to learn that he would be sent for trial, on 5 June 1810, before Lord Ellenborough in the Court of King's Bench. Tomlins and Gullifer, in order to back up their false accusation, ransacked the Police Office to find any paperwork they could use against Harriott. The absurd indictment that resulted was 55 feet long, consisting of 53 spurious counts, which nonetheless involved alleged malversation or embezzlement by Harriott of several thousands of pounds.

All of the charges were dismissed, except one. He had not signed some invoices for work done by his own pump factory to combat water seepage in the basement of the Thames Police Office. It was not underhandedness – everybody in the building knew he was involved with the contract – but misplaced vanity, not wanting his name associated with common manual work. That was no defence. He was found guilty of this single misdemeanour, the jury adding to their verdict that it was done 'without any corrupt motive'. Unfortunately, the judge having retired from the courtroom, the Clerk of the Court recorded this wrongly as 'guilty of the charge of withholding a name' and omitted the jury's rider acquitting Harriott of criminality. So he was fined. An affidavit had to be made out later to amend this injustice.

Leading defence counsel, Mr. J. A. Parks, K.C., who had not met Harriott before, was so impressed by his sterling character, and obvious innocence of corruption, that he returned his fee. The Secretary of State wrote to inform Harriott that His Majesty the King commanded him to resume as Resident Magistrate of the Thames Police. Harriott was vindicated. He was reinstated on 7 July 1810, but now his naval lieutenant son, who had been captured by an Italian Piedmontese frigate, was paroled in London pending payment of a ransom – the lawyer's unused fee paid it. After Harriott's lengthy suspension, without pay, he had no money and on 29 October he wrote to the Secretary of State, describing his plight, and begging for help to support him and his family in their reduced circumstances. It had been another severe test for this doughty man.

CHAPTER TEN

Murder

"The land police can only be made effective in the fast-growing Metropolis if it is made into a preventive system... It is not, however, the being liable to punishment (though convicted,)... so much as the almost certainty of detection, by the vigilance of Police-Officers..."
(John Harriott)

So inadequate were the Police Offices ashore that the Thames Police found themselves more and more often deployed on land at the direction of the Secretary of State. When, in 1810, Sir Francis Burdett (a popular people's champion) was briefly imprisoned in the Tower for a breach of Parliamentary privilege, one of the Magistrates had to remain on duty all night. His colleagues were required to leave addresses where they could be contacted in an emergency, and fifty Marine Police Constables went to reinforce various locations, in case Burdett's supporters caused disturbances. In the same year trouble arose between American, Portuguese and Greek seamen, and a threatened dock strike aggravated matters. Four people were arrested and charged with riotous behaviour and three days later the Magistrates eased any remaining tension by exercising their power to close all the public houses in the area.

Along any Limehouse or Wapping thoroughfare, every other doorway led into a tavern or brothel that never closed. Squalid Elizabethan houses, roofs almost touching, stood either side of a central open gulley that ran with human sewage to the river. The stink of these unpaved, slimy streets was washed away only when it rained. In gloomy side alleys, thugs with coshes and knives lurked; and rough but apparently ready women lured hopeful sailors into them, where they were attacked, robbed and abandoned – often badly hurt. There were areas where, it was said, an armed Constable dared not go; yet, inured to the seediness and danger, well-off families resided amid this squalor. Slums were not then separate places, prosperity and desperate poverty living next-door to one another; so, in 1811, rich and poor alike were terrified by the Ratcliffe murders.

At midnight on Saturday, 7 December a family named Marr was found battered to death in their home at 29 Ratcliffe Highway. The draper and his wife, their infant son and a shop boy, all lay dead in a bloody mess. A ripping chisel – the type used by ships' carpenters – and a maul were found near Mr Marr. This slaughter had occurred in the short time it took the live-in maid to go out and buy some oysters for their supper from a nearby shop. Nothing had been taken, in fact £160 in cash and notes was still in the house.

Public horror had hardly subsided when, on the Thursday night twelve days later, an almost naked man, shouting "They are murdering the people in the house," escaped down knotted sheets from a second-floor window of the King's Arms pub in New Gravel Lane near Ratcliffe Highway. A constable and several neighbours arrived to find the lifeless body of the 72-year-old publican Williamson. His throat was cut, a leg broken, his skull severely fractured. An iron crowbar was lying at his side. In the parlour were Mrs Williamson and her maid, both dead with throats cut and skulls fractured.

Wapping was soon in an uproar; fire bells were rung and a voluntary militia turned out. The Marine Police made a house-to-house search, while colleagues on the river stopped boats and questioned their occupants. The Thames Magistrates circulated a description of the publican's watch which might have been taken by the killer.

These seven violent deaths in less than a fortnight unnerved the City and appalled the whole country. The government had, after the Marr murders, offered a reward of £50 to find the killer, but this was doubled, then raised again to £500. Harriott impulsively offered a further reward for information about three suspects seen loitering near Marr's shop just prior to the crimes – and was promptly reprimanded by the Home Secretary. He apologised in writing, promising to curb his zeal, but averring his determination to track down the killers. One hundred and twenty guineas was the official reward after the Williamson deaths – one hundred for the murderer's conviction, and a further twenty for information about the ripping chisel, maul and crowbar. With nationwide revulsion at such butchery, the authorities were under pressure to catch the killers (thought to be a gang). Forty indiscriminate arrests were made and even Marr's brother was suspected for a time.

Then the landlord of the Pear Tree public house provided a crucial lead. One of his lodgers, having read a description of the maul, recalled seeing a room-mate named John Williams with it shortly before the murders. He told the publican, who passed the story on to the Thames Office. Harriott sent some officers to investigate and they arrested Williams who, when searched, was found to have a bloodstained knife in his waistcoat pocket. Before committal proceedings and consequent trial by judge and jury could resolve his guilt or innocence, he hanged himself in his cell at Coldbath Fields Prison. The body was later carted publicly to the crossroads at Cannon Street, and there between 12 noon and 1 pm it was thrown into a pit, a stake driven through the heart, then buried.

The Ratcliffe murders exposed the useless old nightwatchmen, known as 'Charlies', who spent their duty time boozing and snoozing. All those in Shadwell were summarily dismissed. At Wapping, sixteen extra men were appointed but these were armed and able-bodied. The Thames Magistrates undertook for their Constables to supplement these street patrols when necessary; so peace-keeping policemen became accepted in the locality. But England,

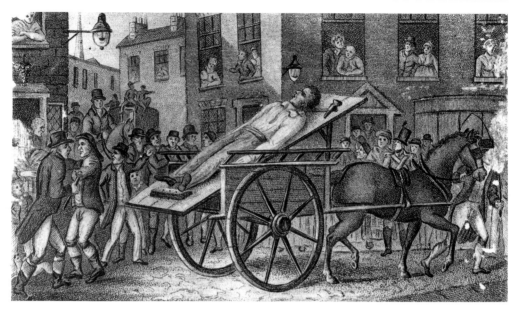

9. The body of John Williams, who hanged himself in his cell when under arrest for the seven Ratcliffe Highway murders in December 1811.

unlike France, would remain for eighteen more years a country with no real police force, and apt to be perversely proud of the fact. One commentator, John William Ward, wrote to his sister: "They have an admirable police in Paris but they pay for it dear enough. I had rather half a dozen people's throats should be cut in Ratcliffe Highway every three or four years than be subject to domiciliary visits, spies, and all the rest..."

John Harriott remained the linchpin of the Thames Office until the end of 1816, when he retired aged 71, stricken with cancer. The following year he died messily in the bath at his house in Burr Street, Spitalfields, from self-inflicted stab wounds. As suicide was then a criminal act, one that shamed the deceased, an admirably compassionate jury concluded it must have been death by natural causes. His grave is in the churchyard of St Mary and All Saints, Great Stambridge, in Essex, a short walk from the family home of Broomhills by the River Roach. There is a commemorative plaque to him inside the church on the west wall. Two years later Patrick Colquhoun retired, almost penniless due to his frequent contributions to charity, and he died on 25 April 1820. A memorial placed in St Margaret's Church, adjoining Westminster Abbey, outlines his many unpaid initiatives and concludes: 'His mind was fertile in conception, kind and benevolent in disposition, bold and persevering in execution.' The names Colquhoun and Harriott had been synonymous with the Marine Police for almost twenty years and they would survive for two centuries. But change was imminent.

CHAPTER ELEVEN

Takeover

"I know nothing at all of the Thames Police; and they may not exist for anything I know of. I find that within a period of two years, notwithstanding our imperfect jurisdiction, from having no communication with the police of the river, that we have apprehended offenders in thirty-seven cases of offences committed on the river."

(A Superintendent of the Metropolitan Police before a House of Commons Committee, 1838)

Harriott would have approved of his successor, Thomas Richbell. He too was an ex-naval officer, then 54 years old, who remained at Wapping until he died in office at the age of 71. He established in 1817 a station aboard an old naval warship, the *Port Mahon*, moored off Somerset House downstream from Waterloo Bridge, which became known as the Upper Station. The same year authorised revenue expenditure rose to £8,300. As an incentive to be vigilant, Surveyors and Constables still received a share of convicted offenders' fines and consequently the magistrates tended to fine (heavily too) rather than imprison. A Danish captain complained to the Home Office when he was fined £2 (quite why, I do not know) for distributing oranges to his crew.

Gangs forced downstream by the presence of the new Marine Police had taken to boarding incoming East India Company ships off Northfleet and Gravesend when crews were being paid-off. They sold the seamen alcoholic drinks, stirred them up to drunken mutiny and amid the confusion looted stores and cargoes. So prevalent was this that Police cutters sailed as far as the Nore to prevent these 'liquor men' getting aboard.

Thames officers did duty at the Coronation of George IV, and the King's private secretary Lord Sidmouth afterwards wrote to them;

> "I am commanded by the King to convey to you His Majesty's most gracious and entire approbation for the exemplary conduct of the Magistrates and Peace Officers on the day of his Royal Coronation, whereby not only the peace of the City of Westminster was preserved, but order and regularity were maintained to a degree seldom, if ever, equalled...."

These were not empty words. Ceremonial events – even of this importance

– were usually marred by disturbances and violence.

In the tenth year of George IV's reign, when the Act authorising the Thames Office finally expired, Sir Robert Peel was at last able to establish a paid and uniformed police force for the Metropolis. The Metropolitan Police Act 1829 applied to a radius of about seven miles from the centre of London, excluding the City. Command of the Force, under the Home Secretary, was initially through the joint control of two Commissioners, Colonel Charles Rowan and Richard (later Sir Richard) Mayne. It did not at first affect the River Police who were allowed to go on independently. They now had three stations: the Thames Office (or Middle Station) at Wapping; the *Port Mahon* (the Upper Station); and a small house (the Lower Station) on the riverside at Blackwall; with a fleet totalling some fifteen boats, three of which constantly patrolled between London Bridge and Deptford.

In 1831 King William IV and Queen Adelaide went in State by river to open John Rennie's new London Bridge. Influential free-loaders invaded the Upper Station, to see something of the royal progress, and Magistrates Ballantine and Richbell wrote afterwards to Lord Melbourne at Whitehall seeking the sum of £8 19s. 7d (perhaps £500 today):

> "...expenses incurred on board the *Port Mahon* on that occasion for Visitors that could not be very well refused and for whom refreshments were ordered – should this charge be at all objectionable the Magistrates will cheerfully take it upon themselves."

His Lordship duly authorised this reimbursement. However his budget was not limitless. About the same time, after a request to fill the vacancy left by a waterman who had died, Lord Melbourne queried if the number of Surveyors could be reduced. Whatever the outcome, by 1832 the river between London Bridge and Greenwich was policed by one Principal Surveyor, nine Surveyors and thirty Watermen; upriver was an Inspecting Surveyor with five Surveyors and eighteen Watermen; and at Blackwall were another Inspecting Surveyor, three Surveyors and nine Watermen.

Since the turn of the century, while the Magistrates' jurisdiction increased, their powers to deploy the manpower had been eroded. The Government, which now paid for the River Police, increasingly told them not only what to do but how to do it, and local initiatives surrendered to central bureaucracy. The Magistrates, in an urgent memorandum to Whitehall dated 16 June 1832, enquired if their Surveyors had the power to search for and seize unlawful gunpowder. (Harriott would never have asked!) A reply the same day confirmed that, in view of the danger arising from ships carrying explosives and even loaded guns among crowded shipping in the Port, they should go ahead.

The old Wapping Office was deteriorating. Repair costs increased and its plumbing, which drew water (sewage and all) from the Thames, always froze in winter. For years the Magistrates had complained to the Secretary of State that the prisoners' quarters were unsuitable: men were kept in a room about nine feet by eight feet, next to a smelly lavatory; women were confined in a small room, although the ceiling was higher, with no outside light or air. Justice Ballantine, generally calm and agreeable, was so annoyed by the shouting and swearing that came through the thin partition from the public rooms that in 1833 he moved the library to an upstairs room – and was promptly admonished by Lord John Russell for not applying in writing for permission to do so.

The unique identity of the Marine Police was about to disappear for ever. With the creation of a Metropolitan Police Force, two discrete law enforcement agencies made little sense. The Metropolitan Police Act 1839 doubled the Force's reach to fifteen miles from Charing Cross, at the same time quadrupling the square mileage of the Police District, and gave it jurisdiction over the River Thames. After ten years of quasi-independence, the Marine Police was absorbed to become simply Thames Division.

Robert Peel has been called 'Father of the Police', as if he somehow invented them. Police constables – initially detested – were nicknamed Peelers and later (more affectionately) Bobbies. In fact Colquhoun and Harriott's plan was 31 years ahead of his. They showed how it could be done and he appears to have copied them; it cannot have been coincidence that Commissioner Mayne was an Irish barrister while Rowan was a Peninsular and Waterloo veteran. The term 'Peace Officers' too (which policemen and women today still like to use) was first applied to the Marine Police. When Sir Richard Mayne proclaimed in 1829:

> "The primary object of an efficient Police Force is the prevention of crime; the next that of detection and punishment of offenders if a crime is committed..."

he was merely repeating principles laid down by Colquhoun and Harriott. Their waterborne force was the true precursor of the Police ideal.

Part II
CHAPTER TWELVE

Changes

"Except in respect of carrying out their patrolling work in boats
instead of on foot...the Thames Division of the Metropolitan Police differs little
from the other divisions of the force."   (Charles Dickens, Junior)

The first Superintendent of Thames Division was John Evans, who had been Chief Boat Surveyor of the Marine Police since 1821. Surveyors became Inspectors; River Police Sergeants were also called Inspectors (2nd or 3rd class) but only received sergeants' pay. This was a deliberate contrivance. Since 1833 Surveyors had carried Customs warrants with formidable extra powers of search and seizure to combat smuggling and Sergeants were designated Inspectors so that they too could be issued with Customs warrants. This privilege is today still enjoyed by Thames Division Inspectors, but no longer by Sergeants.

The Marine Police brought with them into Thames Division some curious bits and pieces of equipment, relics from their pioneer years: 31 cutlasses; 55 large flint pistols; fifteen pocket percussion pistols; eleven powder horns; ten shot moulds; one musket; six blunderbusses; plus a quantity of rattles and handcuffs. More men were posted to the Division, and the Exchequer granted the Force an extra £20,000 a year to cope with patrolling all of the river within the boundaries of the newly enlarged Metropolitan Police District (M.P.D.).

Within a year of amalgamation, the first uniform was issued. Men previously had only greatcoats with truncheons and sidearms. They objected to dressing like the new Peelers but accepted a nautical style, with a straw hat that was protected in winter by a black canvas cover. Second and third class Inspectors (Sergeants) wore a silver crown on the front of their caps and two similar crowns on their jacket collars. Inspectors had a plain black outfit with a peaked cap, braided coats being the only indication that it was a uniform. After the annual inspection in 1868 an Assistant Commissioner reported that the Constables' open neck was unsuitable – he suggested ties – but he rated excellent their voluntary cutlass drill. (Until at least the 1960s, Thames officers wore soft white shirts inside double-breasted reefer jackets and quaint waistcoats, while their land-based colleagues' necks chafed inside traditional blue ones beneath silver-buttoned tunics. Ashore only Inspectors and above wore white shirts. Now the dress of all is, literally, uniform, except that Thames Division retain their nautical reefer jackets for ceremonial best.)

10. Inspector 'Daddy' Bliss who, with six single constables, lived aboard the Royalist (known facetiously as 'the Abode of Bliss').

11.   Overlooking the Upper Pool, c.1910, from London Bridge.

From the time of their formation, the Constables of the five dockyard divisions had used whistles to summon help, although the older rattles were also provided, and wooden whistles were carried in Thames Division boats. By 1872 some officers, like their shore colleagues, wore them on chains, and drivers of the early launches in the 1890s used a short silver-plated brass whistle.

The Thames Court was moved in 1842 to new premises in Arbour Square, Stepney, but Wapping Police Station remained in a dilapidated state until demolished in 1869. Temporary accommodation coped until a new Station, similar to its predecessor and costing £3,490, appeared in 1872; the adjoining wharf was also leased from Bridewell Hospital for £80 annual ground rent, to serve as a boat repair yard with storage for equipment.

The river too was changing. Steel ships powered by steam replaced wooden craft hampered with rope and canvas. The great waterway, once fairly quiet, now clanked, clattered and hissed with machinery, anchor chains and whistles. Pleasure boats, introduced onto the Thames in 1815, soon ousted Margate hoys as the cheap way to the seaside: they reduced the journey to eight hours, when boats dependent upon wind and tide might take ten or more. Competing for a while with the railways, 60-70 luxurious fast steamers ran from London to Greenwich, Woolwich, Gravesend and coastal resorts, enabling men who worked in London all week to go home by river to Kent and Essex at the weekend. And local penny steamers plied between the piers of the City itself.

12. *The Royalist, last of several naval hulks used as Thames Police Stations, made redundant when Blackwall Police Station was built in 1894.*

The Metropolitan Police Force also took a different, less committed view of the river. When in 1875 the Government once again ordered rowing galleys to patrol downriver off Gravesend to protect the King's stores and Customs officers, the Commissioner agreed only with great reluctance as it was outside the M.P.D.

Several wooden vessels were used as floating Police Stations during the nineteenth century. These included the *Port Mahon* which, worn out in 1836, was replaced by the *Investigator*, an old brig of 121 tons. Another brig, the *Scorpion*, was moored off Blackwall from 1840 until 1864 when she was replaced by the *Royalist*, facetiously known up and down the Division as the 'Abode of Bliss' (after the popular Inspector 'Daddy' Bliss who lived on board with six single Constables). She was the last Station vessel, made redundant when the new Blackwall Station was built in 1894.

By the 1860s licensed watermen who plied for hire were few. One of them told the English journalist Henry Mayhew that he blamed the 120 men employed in the public sector by Customs and by Thames Division. Actually, new bridges and better roads killed the nineteenth-century waterborne taxi trade. The medieval London Bridge had been such an obstacle to navigation that at some states of tide few boatmen dared to shoot the tricky water sluicing through its narrow arches, whereas anyone could use Rennie's new structure. The good times were over for watermen and, Mayhew wrote: "...they were ready to snap at one another for threepence when once they had been careless about a shilling".

In 1873 Constables were divided into four watches, each still of six hours,

13. The crew of No. 27 boat (c.1920) verify a waterman's movements during the hours of darkness.

so arranged that a boat came in every two hours and a fresh crew went out. Thus the river was continuously patrolled day and night by alert police officers reacting and responding to movements of doubtful characters, reports of dead bodies, suicide attempts, ships on fire, drifting vessels and wreckage. They now had twelve hours off between shifts, rather than the exhausting six on and only six off. The new rigid rota meant, however, that in the course of three days an officer was afloat every hour in the twenty four. This no doubt ensured up-to-the-minute local knowledge (highly valued by police officers) but must have upset the individual's biorhythms.

The C.I.D. arrived in 1875 when one Detective Sergeant and three Detective Constables were posted to the Division. Plain clothes officers in a rowing galley were shown on the duty rota as 'nondescript' duties, a term still used one hundred years later. River workers were not fooled and could spot a Police boat at the end of a river reach whether or not its crew wore uniform. That hardly mattered, for real detectives, unlike those in books and films, rely more upon what they glean chatting with local informants than from undercover observations; being known is actually an advantage. Charles Dickens junior wondered if the detectives were worthwhile. Arrests, he pointed out, dropped from 107 in 1875 to 88 the following year, then (with the arrival of a fourth officer in 1877) to 73. Convictions also fell from 70 to 57 to 48. The Police point of view, that extra crime fighting probably paid off, was put by Superintendent

14. *Routine police duty in 1938 – checking the paperwork of a waterman dealing in secondhand rope.*

Skeats at the beginning of 1888:

> "Crime has, during the last few years, decreased. It is impossible
> to accurately account for this, but I believe in a great measure this is
> caused by the strict watch kept on the river thieves by the police."

Perhaps it was driven ashore, because the younger Dickens also remarked that the land Divisions of Stepney, Lambeth, Southwark and Greenwich showed no similar decrease. Most of them had more crime, not less. Scotland Yard too seems periodically to have doubted the need for C.I.D. officers familiar with river lore. More than once they were taken away, leaving all major crimes to be dealt with by officers at shore stations. In 1917 they disappeared for several years. Then they returned and stayed until 1975, when they were again removed.

Waterloo Pier was owned by the Conservators of the River Thames when the lower portion was leased by Police in 1873 for £25 a year, a rent was reduced in 1900 when a new barge, solely for use by Thames Division, was placed there.

In 1891, after a tenancy of more than a hundred years, Police compulsorily purchased the freehold of the Thames Office and Wapping boatyard from Bridewell Hospital. About this time the street was renumbered and Thames Division's H.Q. acquired its present postal address of 98-100 Wapping High Street.

Towards the end of the century the G.P.O. central telegraph system reached Wapping, the *Royalist* at Blackwall and Waterloo Pier. By 1903-4 some 10,000 telegraph messages had clicked into Wapping from Scotland Yard, to be transcribed letter by letter onto a slate by the Station Officer. It was a tedious process, made doubly so as contact betwen Wapping and Waterloo Pier went via the Yard. Eventually telephones were installed and Thames Division became an integral part of the Metropolitan Police; but the officers themselves would always be a breed apart.

15. *Officers at Waterloo Pier (c.1950) wore white shirts (not the blue of their shore colleagues) and, when they discarded their reefer jackets, revealed a waistcoat peculiar to Thames Division.*

CHAPTER THIRTEEN

Characters

"However difficult and novel may be the circumstances which confront him in the course of his ordinary duties, he has, unless the matter brooks delay, to decide instantly, and on his own responsibility, whether they call or not for his interference. It follows that a great deal of the most difficult work of the Force is left to the initiative and capacity of the humblest unit in each division."
(Royal Commission upon the Duties of the Metropolitan Police, 1906-8)

These 'humblest units' were robust men who pushed off from the river wall, foreshore, steps, or causeways in open rowing galleys to patrol even in the worst of weather. Driving rain, sleet, snow, fog: none of these relieved them from their duty. Wind over tide kicked up a short, steep swell that threw even the 26-foot clinker-built boats about. Downstream from the ancient stone London Bridge, which survived in one form or another until 1831, ferocious eddies could spin a boat around and overturn it. Some of the twenty narrow arches dammed up the stream. Others funnelled it like weirs and through these the ebb-tide poured, dropping several feet. Only resolute oarsmen shot these rapids and going up through them was sometimes impossible.

For many years the only garment issued to the men was a greatcoat, although they also wore home-made tow (or toe) bags, which were waist-high sacks to keep their legs and feet warm. These were replaced by tilts or boat aprons. Later still they had large capes and sou'westers. The oarsmen kept warm by their exertions, sometimes shedding their jackets, as they pulled the heavy boats through the water. The Surveyor, holding the rudder lines, could only sit and shiver.

Exposure finally weakened even the hardiest. Henry Larwell, a first class Waterman Constable, had served afloat, six hours on and twelve off, for thirty years when he was declared medically unfit at the age of 66. His medical certificate declared he suffered from dropsy (swollen tissues due to retention of fluid) and partial loss of sight. He was worn out by length of service and quite unable to perform further duty. What surely kept such men at their oars was the bonus, one tenth of the value of all stolen goods recovered, or a percentage of an offender's fine. When this was discontinued, so that the whole amount went to the Receiver, a letter of protest on behalf of the men was sent by the Magistrates.

For half a century a family named Judge served within the Division, the first of them enrolling in 1807.   Biblical names were handed down from father to son, so there was always a couple of Joshuas and a Rubin or two. Twenty years later there were three Surveyors and two Waterman Constables, all related Judges, and upon amalgamation the Metropolitan Police acquired four Inspectors (previously Surveyors) named Judge; two were at Wapping with a couple of brothers aboard the *Port Mahon*. One of the latter – Joshua – later took charge of the Upper Station and, when he retired with thirty years service in 1857, the Secretary of State agreed to the rare award of a half-pay annual pension in the sum of £57. The last of the dynasty, George Judge, retired in 1885. The younger men switched to soldiering, which, between the Boer War and the Great War, seems to have wiped out that entire male generation.

Arthur Venables joined Thames Division on Christmas Eve 1867, aged 26, and saw the *Princess Alice* raised from the river bed after she was sunk with the loss of over 600 lives. He retrieved the house flag of the City of London Steamship Company from the forepart of the wreck; and when he died in 1925, aged 84, this memento passed to his grandson who, almost a hundred years after it was assumed lost, gave it to the Thames Police Museum at Wapping.

Henry John Lediard went into the Navy young, manning topsails around

16. Henry Lediard

17. Sergeant 34 'Thames' Hollands on 17 November, 1915, the day he was 'cast' medically unfit. He died the next year.

Cape Horn, before he joined the Metropolitan Police and transferred to Thames Division in 1877. While at Waterloo Pier he took the stand-by boat away single-handed to rescue a woman who had jumped off the bridge, hauling her water-sodden mass inboard over the roller fitted to the stern especially for that purpose. Having resuscitated and landed her, he secured his patient onto the hand ambulance (a stretcher, with broad leather straps, mounted on a two-wheeled costermonger's barrow) and – still unaided – pushed her to Westminster Hospital.

Lediard was a man admired by his colleagues: a member of the Metropolitan Police Christian Association, and one of the first Thames Officers to obtain (in 1882) a St John's Ambulance first aid certificate. Old lags too respected him. His wife proudly told how once, when he was shopping with her in The Cut street market at Blackfriars, a tough grabbed hold of him ... but then released him, saying; "It's you. D'you know, if you 'adn't spoken the truth in Court, I'd 've 'ad a longer sentence." Promoted Inspector in 1888 and transferred to Wapping, Henry Lediard retired on completion of 25 years service and became an active member of the Police Pensioners' Association. As an old man he was often seen working in soup kitchens for the homeless or giving out clothing to needy children. Three of his sons became policemen: the youngest – Edward 'Foxy' Lediard – joined Thames Division where, in 1911, he revived a person from the river and was awarded a Bronze Medal by the Royal Humane Society.

The only twentieth-century father-and-son sequence was Superintendent William 'General' Gordon and Sergeant Peter Brian Gordon, who between them served commendably from 1940 to 1993. Ill-health cruelly took both men before retirement.

P.C. Mackenzie was the holder of a Polar Medal, having served with Captain Robert Falcon Scott in the Antarctic. He became a Mounted Branch officer; but then one day he looked over the river wall, liked what he saw, and transferred to Thames Division.

A popular man must have been P.C. Bond who lived with his father, the licensee of the Waterman's Arms public house, just two doors along from the Station. In 1890 he plunged into the river after an escaping prisoner, whom he caught, but then died from pneumonia in June that year.

The Roll of Honour at the rear of this book, listing the names of Thames officers killed on duty or active military service, does *not* record the far larger number of officers – like Henry Larwell and P.C. Bond – who died, were injured, made ill or simply worn out by their arduous Police duty afloat. By the mid-nineteenth century a quarter of a million sewage outlets drained directly into the River Thames, which carried an increasingly concentrated load of human excreta and other infectious filth up and down with the tides. Repeated cholera epidemics killed tens of thousands of Londoners. In 1861 Queen Victoria's beloved Albert died of typhoid fever. If the Prince Consort – remote upriver at Windsor Castle – could not escape disease resulting from lack of public hygiene, then boat crews in direct daily contact with the source of such infection were dreadfully vulnerable. Individual officers whose health was ruined were unkindly 'cast' as medically unfit for further Police duty. The photograph of Police Sergeant Hollands is included as a poignant reminder of all those men. After seven years in the Army, he served 21 years in Thames Division and in 1915, obviously ill, he posed in his best uniform for this studio portrait (p. 58) on the very day that he was cast. He died the following year.

The premature death of another officer, followed by action from his hardup widow, resulted in a better lot for Police dependants. Michael Moody joined Thames Division in 1905 and was one of the first motorboat drivers. In 1910 he fell into the river and was sick for several months with pneumonia. As no money was then paid for time off work, apart from a small sick club payment, his young wife and he were supported by friends. He returned to duty and was at the Sidney Street seige. Still unwell, he stayed in the Division when war began in 1914,

18. P.C. Michael Moody, whose premature death in 1919 from ill-health ultimately secured pensions for police widows.

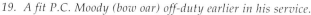

19. A fit P.C. Moody (bow oar) off-duty earlier in his service.

walking daily to Wapping from Deptford, returning off night duty to collect his pay, and setting out again for the Station whenever a Police whistle or Boy Scout bugle signalled the start of an air raid. Such commitment by a Police officer was unremarkable, since whole time to Police duty was then demanded. During all of his thirteen years service he was granted just one day's leave, Christmas Day 1917. Early in 1918, the Divisional Surgeon placed Michael Moody in the Police Nursing Home at Hove and he never returned to duty. Before the year was over he was required to resign, aged 39, medically unfit. He went home and died three months later from pulmonary tuberculosis. His widow Marion ('Maisy') had to borrow money to bury him and a gratuity paid later by Scotland Yard barely met the funeral expenses. She was left almost destitute.

Discontent over pay and conditions led in 1919 to the only national Police strike. Afterwards Maisy Moody addressed the newly formed Police Federation on behalf of Police dependants and received a standing ovation. Heartened, she went on to talk to anyone who would listen about the suffering endured by many others like herself, even persuading her M.P. to ask a question in Parliament. When the Police Pensions Act 1921 went onto the statute book, it included widows' pensions; but the benefit was only back-dated to April 1919, not quite far enough to include Michael Moody's death. She never received the benefit she helped win for others and was penniless.

Two Thames officers lived to be one hundred years old. Lewis Henry Keaton did not die until September 1970, at the age of 101, but had joined the Metropolitan Police in 1891 and retired from Thames Division as an Inspector in

20. Ex-Thames Inspector, Lewis Henry Keaton on his 100th birthday in 1970.

1917. P.C. Bullion, who early in his service rowed Inspector Keaton around, was the other. He was a Scots Guardsman who fought with General Kitchener at the Battle of Omdurman in the Sudan and later in the South African Boer War. He joined Thames Divison on the personal recommendation of Edward VII, and after twelve years policing the river he was recalled to the Colours at the outbreak of World War I and served as a Metropolitan Police drill sergeant with the East Lancashire Regiment throughout those hostilities. He returned to Thames Division shortly afterwards and was posted engineer, or boat driver, aboard the launch *Renavire*. George Bullion retired in 1927, to serve in the Home Guard during World War II, and was President of the Thames Police Association for fourteen years. He too was 101 years old when he died.

One of the bravest men to go afloat in Thames Divison must surely have been Sergeant Sidney Woolcott. He was in a team of Second World War frogmen who undertook a hazardous Far East operation to sink Japanese ships in Phuket Harbour. Wearing unreliable re-breathing apparatus (no giveaway bubbles when they exhaled), riding astride temperamental submersibles, they carried limpet mines to enemy targets. Asphyxiation and drowning from technical failures in their own equipment were very real risks for these 'human torpedos', while the Japanese had promised to cut out the eyes and testicles of captured charioteers. Surviving his mission, he clamped explosives to the barnacle-encrusted bilge keels of the 5,000 ton *Sumatra Maru*, and was safely back aboard his own ship in time to hear the target blow up. Sidney Woolcott was awarded the Distinguished Service Medal. Entering Thames Division after the war he must have found the Police duty boat a cosy berth.

It used to be that most Thames Division officers had served in either the Merchant or Royal Navy, or at least one of the other Armed Forces. That is no longer so and their backgrounds are diverse, except that few Freemen of the River ever seem to have chosen a second career that led them into Thames Division. Two ex-lightermen did. Divisional Superintendent Ronald Main, who retired in 1972, and P.C. Kevan Keefe who joined the Force in 1964 and completed his service in 1993, both brought extra aptitude and experience to their work.

Inspector Dick Whitworth, who retired in 1995, chronicled river policing for more than 25 years in a series of amusing cartoons. Many of them recall incidents best appreciated only by those who were involved; but the trio included in this book aptly depict the way the Division has evolved.

CHAPTER FOURTEEN

Oars to Engines

"...us boys...found the body of a woman in the sand and mud...we saw the three policemen rowing and an inspector in the stern and we shouted and shouted... A rope was tied around her right shoulder and armpit and she was towed away by the rowers." (William Pearson: on his Rotherhithe boyhood, c.1916)

Police motorboats are a twentieth-century development. Galleys were used from 1798 until rowing patrols ended in 1925, and the last one was not sold until 1931. The Commissioner hired a steam launch – the *Mahseer* – to patrol the Pool during a watermen's strike, and some were then acquired in the 1880s, but not until 1912 was an internal combustion engine tried. Diesel engines were adopted around 1920.

The first Thames steam tug with its tall funnel trailing smoke and smuts began work in 1801 and, if a Surveyor was agreeable, Police oarsmen soon learned to hang off the end of a tow of barges going their way, for pulling upriver against a strong ebb tide required a strenuous and sustained effort; while to round a sharp bend like Tripcock Point opposite Barking Creek, without being swept back by the force of the stream, could take several attempts (even rowing randan). A randan skiff was propelled by three men using four oars. Bow and stroke wielded a single blade each, while the third man sat on the centre thwart with a pair of sculls. Surveyors – later first class Inspectors – commanded randan skiffs, giving them more mobility to supervise. Second and third class Inspectors (Sergeants) only merited two oarsmen.

An open boat was no place to fight, for, if an offender resisted arrest, all could end up struggling in the water. "Are you coming quietly?" was asked by River Police Surveyors long before shore officers had occasion to do so.

Boat building was contracted out to Martin of Greenwich. The specification required prime English oak, with grown knees, free from sap and of the best workmanship, the outside of each boat to be dressed with resin and tallow. Some say that galleys working above London Bridge were varnished, whereas those below were painted black. There was a quaint boat mending shed next to the Police Office at Wapping; while, for small jobs, the boats were simply brought alongside the river wall and allowed to ebb dry on the hard (foreshore). Rowing galleys were later lifted out of the water and into a boatyard for major work by means of a Weston purchase run out from the building on an H-girder.

21. Inspector (third class) Plumb and his crew pose in 1899; three men with four oars was known as rowing randan.

Patrols were extended in 1804 when a sailing cutter was bought to supervise the longer and wider downriver reaches. The crew's main job was to protect the King's stores at Sheerness and other Royal Dockyards but they also prevented prize-fighting, sheep-stealing and smuggling along the Kent and Essex shores. The boat was dirty (that is, it shipped a lot of water) and disliked for that reason. When sold in 1808, the replacement was a massive 18-ton Customs cutter crewed by an Inspector and eight Constables who lived aboard for two weeks at a stretch. This too was duly replaced by smaller craft, the *Antelope* (1819) and the *Spray* (1870). When the *Spray* was written off, following a collision with a steam launch, it became a floating Police station at Cory's Jetty, Erith, and there it remained, apart from a spell at Woolwich in 1883, until 1892 when a wooden cabin was erected on the shore. The present brick building with its gable end facing the river was opened on 1 November 1908, to be fully manned by an Inspector, two Sergeants and eight Constables – effectively the crew of the Customs cutter of exactly 100 years earlier.

Steamships had been part of the scene for more than sixty years, yet Surveyors were still being rowed around by Watermen Constables, when at 7.35 pm on 3 September 1878, the iron screw ship *Bywell Castle* ran down the passenger steamer *Princess Alice* in Gallions Reach. It was the worst ever Thames shipping disaster. The small paddle ship with up to 800 day-trippers aboard (and overloaded) was returning from the coast, via Sheerness and Gravesend, to Swan Pier at London Bridge. She broke in two and sank within minutes. Only 150 survived. In all that has been written about this tragedy not much is mentioned of the work done by Thames Division. Every officer and boat was used to recover over 600 dead and decomposing bodies, many those of women and children.

22. A rare photograph (c.1900) of a Marine Police galley patrolling in King's Reach and approaching the old Waterloo Bridge.

They also had to oversee in dismal sheds the dockside identification by relatives. Superintendent Alstin reported afterwards;

> "The Police continued their exertions when labourers and others had refused to perform their loathsome work, although tempted with high wages."

An inquest and a lengthy Board of Trade enquiry followed. At these hearings the Woolwich Coroner and other officials commented upon the inadequacy of rowing galleys for Police duty. They pointed out that the river was now busy with vessels under power and recommended that Thames Division should have steam launches. But it was the mid-1880s before Police took delivery of two of these, one for use above London Bridge and other below it. The first was the *Rover* which was bought secondhand from the Isle of Dogs and could do six knots. Next was the custom-built teak 30-foot *Alert*, later replaced by the steel-hulled *Chowkidar* (Night Watchman) with the Alert's engine. By their 100th birthday in 1898 Thames Division had a further eight steam pinnaces or launches to supplement 28 rowing galleys. One of these, the *Sir Richard Mayne*, arrived with an engineer named Mitchell, lent by the boat's builder for three months to teach running and maintaining of the craft. He stayed for nearly thirty years.

George Mitchell became the Division's first and only Sergeant Engineer and the officer in charge of the Carpenters' Repair Department. He designed and

23.   *The yellow funnelled steam launch Watch, the largest ever commissioned for Thames Division.*

24.   *The steel hulled steam launch Chowkidar (Night Watchman) alongside the Police pier below the old Waterloo Bridge.*

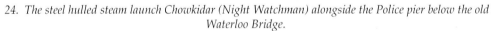

25. *The Howard, first of the custom-built police motor boats (c.1907).*

built a single-cylinder, two-stroke, petrol/paraffin engine and obtained permission to fit it into a rowing galley. It was not a success. Rated less than two horse-power, it pushed the boat through the water at no more than four knots, not enough to punch the ebb up through London Bridge without the help of oars. Oars were also needed when it failed altogether, which it often did.

Sir John Thorneycroft came downriver to Wapping from his Chiswick shipyard, looked at Mitchell's engine, and devised his own version called the Handy Billy. The first galley converted with it capsized during trials. The boat was top-heavy, the inboard engine mounted too high, and it was promptly nicknamed the 'Irish Molly' (wryly referring either to the terrorist Molly Maguire or simply to a woman with a big bust). Six galleys were fitted with the engine and all were unstable at first; only by trial and error was the right balance achieved. Mitchell was awarded £10 by the Police Commissioner for his initiative and Thorneycroft did even better with his Handy Billy which enjoyed worldwide sales.

Still, in 1913, a Sergeant was drowned when his motorised rowing galley was overpowered by the current and swept under moored barges. Critics said such boats were not fit for the Serpentine, let alone the Thames tideway, and conversions were finally abandoned. Working under Mitchell was P.C. Frederick Moore, a Constable-Carpenter, who had served his time as a joiner in Devonport Dockyard before transferring to Thames Division in 1886. He helped build the first Police designed duty boat but it was too heavy and unsuitable for the job. So about 1906-7 tenders were invited for powered boats.

The first of the custom-built craft, slightly larger and stronger than the galleys, was to work upstream from Richmond sluices. As the Thames Conservancy, whose section of river this was, required every vessel to have a name (not merely a fleet number) it was called the *Howard*. Although to Police specifications this design too proved faulty and unreliable, oars still having to be carried for emergency use.

By the first quarter of the twentieth century the Division's fleet was very mixed. At Blackwall Police Station for example, about 1913, there were, as well as galleys, two very different motorboats. One was a rowing conversion but the second was purpose-built with a torpedo boat forecastle. There were also two larger launches: the *Sir Richard Mayne II*, the first petrol/paraffin launch, from J. Samuel White in 1910, which backfired viciously when started and issued clouds of dense black smoke as well as engine fumes that upset passengers and crew; the other was the yellow-funnelled steam launch *Watch*, the largest ever commissioned for the Division – 47 feet overall with a 9' 6" beam - built by Watkins in Bow Creek. These bigger boats could not simply be drawn up onto the hard. They had to have mooring piles or buoys fixed into the river bed. A small coal bunker was added for the steam launches and pinnaces. The fuel for the boats with internal combustion engines was originally delivered in two-gallon cans, before the installation of storage tanks with fuel pumps in 'dummy' (dumb barge) pontoons at stations.

The early motor boats were open and extremely unpleasant in bad weather. The men sat, soaked and frozen (at least the oarsmen had kept active and warm before) and the engines were not wholly dependable. Such conditions afloat would not be alleviated for twenty years. Still, by the end of 1914, there was a fleet of thirty custom-built motor boats. Upriver, from Wapping to Staines Bridge, 22-foot boats were used; downstream 27-footers were employed. Crews too were changing.

"Just think – one day we'll have fibreglass duty boats with twin screw turbo charged diesel engines!"   *(Cartoon by ex-Inspector, Richard Whitworth)*

CHAPTER FIFTEEN

Motorboats

"Those Thames Division officers of today, who are RIB* trained and have experienced their first winter in open boats...have some understanding of the harsh conditions experienced by their predecessors, who worked the rowing galleys and sailing cutters of the Marine Police of Nelson's day."
(Peter Andrews, Editor, *Thames Police Journal*, 1994)

The Inspectors and Sergeants of Thames Division, like the Marine Police Surveyors before them, were rowed about the river beats, steering their galleys with rudder lines. Motorboats, when they arrived, needed different handling. The supervising officer had a tiller or wheel and some Constables were sent to the Royal Navy at Sheerness for a course in the basics of driving the motorboat engine. The third man became a deckhand.

Going afloat in an early motorboat was a complicated business. The P.C. driver set about starting (say) a Kelvin engine with a handle inserted into the crankshaft. This had to be turned without any guides and, as it was near the bottom of the boat, he usually skinned his knuckles. Still, he was paid 6d (2½p) a day extra for his expertise. The engine consisted of two separate blocks, each of two cylinders and carburettors with spring-loaded air intakes. He primed and started the engine with petrol, poured via the air intakes, before changing to paraffin for routine running. Any officer who forgot this switch-over quickly emptied the meagre half-gallon petrol tank. When the engine failed it might not start again, leaving the boat helplessly riding the tide, until the crew were either able to take a safe mooring turn somewhere or got out the oars. This rigmarole had to be done in all weathers, so the engineer carried his own set of sparking plugs, which he would pre-heat by soaking them in petrol and setting fire to them. He guarded his plugs jealously, removing them at the end of each tour of duty, hence the burnt holes in his boat coat pockets. He also carried a heart-shaped oil can which, in an emergency, might provide extra power if he poured more petrol through the air intakes.

The deckhand shipped a pitchfork-type mast, then lit and positioned temperamental oil navigation lamps. After 1907 these were acetylene. He checked loose items of boat's gear, including a standby set of oars lashed inside the gunwales, which were to pull the boat out of danger when the engine failed

*rigid inflatable boat

26. The Division's first petrol-paraffin launch, Sir Richard Mayne II, at J. Samuel White's Yard, Southampton, in 1910

– but they were almost useless. The crutches (or rowlocks) were on the inboard side of four inch wide gunwales so, as soon as an oar touched the water and power was applied, it jumped out. These boats were no longer made to be rowed.

Casting off when his skipper ordered, the deckhand quickly slid into his toe bag or he wrapped a rectangular sheet of waterproof oilskin or rubber with a serge lining, known as a 'tilt' (or apron), around his lower half. Before engines only Surveyors or Inspectors needed tilts; from 1902 every crew member was issued one. This protective layer, over boat coat or cape topped off with a sou'wester rain hat, was indispensable. The river-wise Sergeant would take the tiller on the lee side aft, leaving the deckhand as a shield on his weather side, so even a slight popple on the water meant a wet watch afloat (by now generally eight hours, not six), and much of the water shipped by the long, low and open boat drenched the exposed deckhand.

The coxswain called out instructions ("Ahead", "Astern", and "Slow", "Half" or "Full Speed") and the driver-engineer, comparatively snug amidships abaft his warm engine, manipulated gears and revs. A code of hand signals was evolved, too, which worked well except when, very occasionally, with an unpopular skipper, it could be deliberately misunderstood.

The launch *Renavire* was a splendid 45-50 foot mahogany petrol/paraffin craft with a 9' 6" beam, purchased for the Police by Major Vitty, Scotland Yard's Engineer, from a private owner on the Clyde. Distinctive features included the row of eleven brass portholes along each side of the low cabin and twin ventilation cowls. It was brought from the west coast of Scotland by ship about Christmas 1920, launched in the London docks, and completed the journey by river to Wapping, where it was put on the hard and made ready by George Mitchell for Police work. Renamed *Vigilant*, the conversion involved removing

27. The mahogany launch Renavire at anchor on 29 December 1920. One of her crew, P.C. Bullion, lived to the age of 101 years.

six bunks and installing a table that seated twelve, a pantry with oil stove cooking and a toilet. The controls for the boat's two 30 hp Renault engines could be worked remotely by one person in the wheelhouse – how all Police boats would one day be – but for some reason (maybe to create a post for an engineer) Mitchell made new controls with a telegraph from the wheelhouse to the engine room. Top speed was about 10 knots.

In 1921 the Government recommended that all rowing patrols should cease but this did not happen immediately. In 1921-2 two more launches were bought by Major Vitty. One was a smart mahogany ex-yacht tender, the other a troublesome double-skinned teak boat called *Katalina*. Too fine in the bilge, it fell over on its side as the tide receded, unless tightly tied to the berth, and once sank unnoticed like this.

28. The driver (or engineer) of these open petrol-paraffin boats was paid an extra 6d (2½p) a day for his expertise

29. A 30-foot wooden duty boat with Perkins P6 marine diesel engine, stems the tide on a misty morning in the Lower Pool (1953)

Other boats to arrive in the 1920s were bought from either the Army or Navy. One, fitted with a diesel engine, was started by screwing a steel bottle of compressed air into the cylinder head. Then, at the jerk of a lever, the released air provided initial compression. Before the process could be repeated, pressure in the container had to be restored by strenuous hand pumping, which was a source of some frustration. But the boat was popular because, once started, it fairly flew along.

George Mitchell, the last policeman in the boat repair yard, retired in 1924. A year later rowing patrols ended. A new *Alert* in 1928, built by Frank Maynard of Chiswick, had a four-cylinder Ailsa Craig 30 hp petrol/paraffin engine capable of 10 knots. Length 31 feet, beam seven feet, draught four feet, it was teak and oak, with pitch pine decks, having a seven feet and two inches saloon with full headroom, a washbasin and lavatory (in the forward chain locker). In 1931 the last rowing galley was sold; and Sergeant Sebborn, boatbuilder/carpenter, was granted a gratuity of ten guineas for designing a new motor launch at Major Vitty's suggestion. Motorboats were now the only way to patrol and do Police work.

Between the wars diesel engines took over Thames Division. No. 14 boat was fitted with a Gardiner engine in June 1926. From 1930 to 1938 other boats had either Parsons or AEC diesel engines fitted, giving them speeds of 14 knots. Then, in 1940, the Osborne-built boats, with Perkins P6 engines rated at 65 hp with 2,000 revs per minute, were adopted as the standard and by 1941 there were six of them. This reliance by Thames Division upon the products of Perkins Engines Ltd., of Peterborough, has worked for more than half a century and it continues today. Coxswains gained complete control of the boats via handy gear and throttle levers. But they still had no cabins.

CHAPTER SIXTEEN

Cabins and Call Signs

Patrol boats are linked to all Metropolitan Police radio channels, so there is a co-ordinated response with land-based officers. The Division also monitors marine radio communications on the river, to stay completely informed at all times.

(Metropolitan Police Force, Directorate of Public Affairs, leaflet, 1986)

Before radios, boats' crews contacted Stations fairly easily in the day time when officers simply landed at a wharf or pier and asked to use the telephone; landing places at night were fewer and telephones not always accessible. It was harder for the Station Officer to contact a boat, as he relied upon the goodwill of wharf managers and piermasters to intercept boats and ask the officer in charge to ring the Station. When this failed a Police boat could be close to a serious incident and know nothing about it.

There were 28 open motor boats based at five Stations in 1933. All were 26 feet long, with boxed engines amidships and their helms aft. Crews in these boats sat on solid wooden chairs which, because they were not fixed down, swayed and shifted (even fell over) in a swell. The tough kapok-filled canvas cushions issued to each boat as buoyancy aids for emergencies were used unofficially to make them comfortable. The large diesel engine in some of the 1940 boats left little space for the third wooden chair, which was squeezed between engine and gunwale, so that its occupant was subjected to almost unbearable noise and vibration.

Contacting boats by wireless telegraphy (W/T) using Morse code had been considered as early as 1927 but no radio set could then do the job. The first boat with a W/T receiver was No. 18 in 1931. Boats with temporary radio equipment were also used at a Greenwich river pageant sometime after that. Then Home Office approval was given in January 1934 for the installation of W/T transmitters and receivers on two boats under construction, and the fitting of receivers (only) in four of the existing boats, for a total estimated cost of £480. The sets were built, and the six boats wired to take them, the problem of the transmitters' weight overcome by using Duralumin mountings instead of brass. The radio despatchers in Scotland Yard's Information Room, who kept track of Police car deployment on large-scale map tables by means of coloured and numbered tokens, now augmented them with new ones for Thames Police boats.

Open boats were not suitable for W/T sets. Removable glass screens forward and side flaps of oilskin or canvas – later made permanent – kept out wind and spray but not the rain. Deckhands and redundant boat drivers/engineers doubled as wireless operators, relying on loudspeakers because headphones were impractical, but it was hard to hear over the noise of the boat's engine. Senior officers, who did not go afloat much – except in their smart and comfortable launches – resisted cabins for those who did. Men would grow soft, they argued ("We never had them."). They would be reluctant to quit a snug cabin to undertake work ("It never did us any harm."). Dozy and inattentive to river traffic, they would be run down and drowned ("They're not as dedicated today as we were"). When cabins were eventually fitted, they were to protect the precious new wireless sets.

The first of several cabin tops was designed and built by P.C. Archie Brown of Blackwall on the 28-foot No. 9 boat. He made another for No. 11, which proved trickier due to the awkward placing of engine and steering wheel. In 1936 they were both inspected, officially approved and adopted as the models for altering other boats. Like P.S. Sebborn, he was awarded ten guineas.

The pounding and vibration of the boats caused many W/T breakdowns and sets were often out of service for repair and hopes of improved efficiency, with boats readily on call, were at first frustrated. Reliability was only gradually achieved, after which the network was extended to cover the section from Wandsworth Bridge to Teddington Lock; the haphazard practice of telephoning to ask piermasters and shore P.C.s to hail passing boats with urgent messages then died out.

In 1935 Scotland Yard changed from W/T to voice transmissions. Radio telephony (R/T) needed high output C.A. Vanderbelt generators and current voltage regulators, with heavy duty NIFE or Nickel Cadmium batteries. In 1941 the Marconi transmitters were replaced by two-way radio, with telephone-type handsets, powered by charger batteries. By 1949 the Division had 33 R/T duty boats with cabins. Perkins marine diesel engines pushed them through the water at nearly fifteen knots. Radical changes in boat design were just about done but these motorboats needed skilled technical maintenance.

CHAPTER SEVENTEEN

Workshops

"It is here that all types of engine repairs, and maintenance...are dealt with, and the hulls and fittings attended to in a manner which ensures the whole fleet being maintained in the highest standard of efficiency.
(Souvenir programme: *Review of the Thames River Police 1798-1949*)

The Division's workshops started by chance when, in 1817, the Thames Magistrates accepted on free loan from the Admiralty the wooden Naval vessel *Port Mahon* and a recruiting barge *Tower*, to serve as floating Police Stations. With each came a boatswain and a ship's carpenter, on half pay, as the ships were part of the Reserve fleet. It was agreed to make up their wages to that of Constables from the Police Fund, if they would keep their vessels shipshape, repair the Police rowing galleys and make new oars when required. After five years the boatswains were no longer needed, but the carpenters were kept on and granted an allowance to buy overalls.

Once it was decided, about 1914, to stop putting engines in rowing galleys, a skilled and dedicated civilian workforce became essential. In 1938 a shipwrights' workshop was established to complement the carpenters' shop. Before World War II the staff totalled just fifteen men but by the end of hostilities there were 32, all under a Chief Engineer, including: three charge hands; four shipwrights; seven carpenters; seven engineers; two electricians; fitters and painters; and a storekeeper; all dedicated to keeping the men of Thames Division afloat and effective. Police boats had regular workshop inspections every 300 hours, when minor maintenance was done, and 600 hours for major overhauls. These periods later lengthened to 400 and 800 hours, with each boat running for about 2,500 hours (just over 100 days) a year.

A 'wim-wom' is something tangled around a boat's screw or prop-shaft. It is the most peculiar Thames term, perhaps echoing the sound, as an unbalanced propellor shakes with an ugly 'whum, whum' noise. Discarded rope, sheets of polythene, animal carcases, motor tyres and barbed wire are just a few of the things that make an engine labour or stop it dead. In the Division's museum at Wapping there is a half-inch diameter iron bar coiled like a giant clock spring, a wim-wom removed from a duty boat. Wim-woms float awash just beneath the surface or are picked up off the riverbed in shallow water; either way a coxswain cannot see them, and they happen in a second. One moment the boat is churning along, the next a violent jolt and the engine stops or acquires a nasty shudder. Sometimes the boat can be restarted and nursed slowly back to the Station under its own power without damage, but often it must be towed. Foul screws are the most numerous causes of breakdowns and crews hope (even quietly pray) one will not occur when – as they often must – they work their boats into precarious places to rescue others in difficulty and danger.

Clearing a wim-wom entails hoisting the stern out of the water with a crane, then cutting the tangle off from a dinghy bouncing beneath the duty boat. When that is impossible the boat has to go to Wapping to be lifted competely out of the water. A wim-wom in 1970 took workshop staff three days with hacksaws and wirecutters to remove; the screw, prop-shaft and rudder were completely hidden within a spring mattress, some blankets, nylon and wire ropes. A further afternoon was spent withdrawing, straightening and refitting the prop-shaft.

New workshops were opened on 25 September 1973 at the disused Morocco & Eagle Sufferance Wharves, just a cobblestone's throw west from where Colquhoun and Harriott had faced and driven off rioting coal heavers: the site had been purchased by Police in 1968, having been derelict for several years. The opening ceremony was performed by the Minister of State at the Home Office, the Rt. Hon. Mark Carlisle, who came downriver in the launch *John Harriott* to be met by the Commissioner of Police and other senior officers. Speeches over, and a plaque uncovered, Chief Engineer Fred Byway showed the dignitaries around. The new boatyard was 200 feet long, 100 feet wide, and jutted – supported on concrete piles – 145 feet out into the river. It could be used at any state of the tide. The 20,000 square feet accommodated boats, engineers, carpenters all on one level. There were offices, stores, a canteen, rest

30. *Tackling a wim-wom (fouled propellor) at Waterloo Pier in the 1960s.*

and drying rooms, and an underground car park at the landward end (with an electrically heated ramp) which could take 30 vehicles.

Designed by the Architect's Department at Scotland Yard, the facility had many novel features, the most eye-catching being the white glass reinforced plastic outer cladding with an abstract relief pattern. Of greater practical value was the 'Synchro-lift' boat hoist. A boat could be guided onto it and lifted out of the water, sitting in a wheeled cradle, then manhandled into the covered workshop. It could also raise boats just clear of the water to remove wim-woms. The lift could cope with up to 15 tons deadweight and a number of the mobile cradles were supplied for different hull profiles. It was the first of its kind in Britain. Because this unique lifting device might be involved in an accident when it was on or in the water, it was, for insurance purposes, registered with Lloyds of London as a ship (Boats could only be lifted from the river into the old boatyard at high tide; then, in the cramped space intended just for rowing galleys, a losing game of workshop Solitaire ensued, in which nothing could be moved until a space was created by first moving something else.)

Once the workshops were relocated, the plan had been for the existing Thames Police Station at 98 Wapping High Street to be demolished and replaced by a new Divisional H.Q. This idea was shelved in 1974. Instead the Edwardian building was given a facelift and the interior renovated. The redundant boatyard became a small covered car park, while the wonderfully eclectic Thames Police Museum came out from hiding in fourth-floor cupboards to be permanently displayed in the abandoned carpenters' workshop.

31. Fred Byway, B.E.M., civilian chief engineer, who in 1978 completed forty years in Thames Division, and a total of fifty years service with the Metropolitan Police.

In 1970 Fred Byway was awarded the British Empire Medal. Illness delayed the presentation but he received it in 1971 from the hand of Lord Lieutenant Field Marshal Sir Gerald Templar. When in 1977 he clocked up 50 years service with the Metropolitan Police, he also became the longest serving member (Police or Civil) in Thames Division. Fred finally hung up his spanners the following year, having been with the River Police for 40 years. Shortly afterwards, the boatyard storekeeper Arthur George Garwood also achieved 40 years in Thames Division and he too received the B.E.M. from the Lord Lieutenant of London, Lord Elworthy, at County Hall.

What was once exclusively Thames Division's boatyard now maintains other Police vehicles. Indeed they outnumber the duty boats, since cost-cutting measures have reduced the fleet and the Workshop Manager needs the extra work from land divisions to justify his existence. Police vans, cars and motorbikes – even the occasional horsebox – jacked up and in pieces, crowd out the Thames boats; while, for the fitters or mechanics too, the demands of Thames Division are an unprofitable distraction. The symbiosis which existed between Thames Police crews and the civilian shipwrights, carpenters and engineers has gone, perhaps for ever, as the talk is now of putting boat maintenance out to tender and contract.

CHAPTER EIGHTEEN

Green Parrots and Other Rarities

*"...I looked up from my river-facing desk and was astonished to see,
powering its way down river...a 1963 fibreglass replica of...a 1930s RAF
Class 200 sea-plane tender bearing the livery of the Thames Police."*
(David Balkham, 1995)

In 1893 the British motorboat pioneer Frederick Simm loaned Thames Division
a Daimler launch. This may have been part of a strategy to overcome the public
prejudice and fear that boats powered by petroleum spirit were liable to explode.
Anyway, the boat worked well. In the early 1900s Hubert Scott-Paine gave the
Division the *Sea Jack*. Built by his British Power Boat Company at Hythe in
Hampshire, it was said he used this fast, hard-chine boat to cross Southampton
Water to where he lived on the east shore, because the trip took ten minutes
instead of over an hour by road in his Bentley car. Any hopes he must have
had for orders from Thames Division went unfulfilled. It might have made
an ideal emergency boat for officers to slip away quickly to an accident, a suicide
or a child bather in difficulties, but it was not strong enough for a working patrol
boat, although it was used for a while by supervising officers. It had a rubbing
strake of rubber which would bind when the boat was berthed on piles athwart
(side on to) the stream. Instead of rising steadily with the flood tide, friction
held it down until it broke free, when it came up in a series of jerks. This pulled
the strake loose from its fastenings and, although alternatives were tried, nothing
lasted long.

Officers had to operate in several different boats, swapping sometimes daily
from one to another. A few were bad – death traps, they said. The handiest
were the 30-footers from the Arun shipyard of Osbornes at Littlehampton, also
the ones built upriver on the Thames by Tough & Henderson, which a capable
coxswain could put anywhere. Officers knew the good and bad characteristics
of every boat in which they patrolled. Two teak-hulled cabin boats built by
Vospers of Portsmouth about 1934, and attached to Blackwall Police Station,
had high foredecks and rounder bottoms than most others in the fleet. Both
rolled a lot but one of them had the best stern gear. Some boats were dirty,
shipping water in rough conditions, others dryer. Quiet boats were preferred
to noisy ones. Some engines died if – still cold – stern gear was engaged; one
or two did the opposite, surging dangerously ahead.

Thames Division's most unloved boat, No. 18, was a steel one. Taken into

32. The mid-1960s Wapping waterside; two fibreglass duty boats (without cabin doors) occupy the upper berth, while the lower wooden boat has been painted grey prior to collection by a new private owner.

service at Waterloo Pier in 1944, it was made by William Osborne. The standard 30 feet long, with eight feet six inches of beam and two feet nine inches draught, the hull was one-eighth inch thick plates welded together and shot-blasted inside and out to stop rust. There was a watertight compartment aft but no other buoyancy. A steel prop-shaft, zinc-coated steel propellor and steel underwater cooling pipes completed this metallic concept craft. Work and the river soon aged it. After only two or three years it went into the boatyard, where the dents were filled with plumber's solder, and it was then sanded down to look less battered and worn. In a short while it was as bad as before. Everyone called it the 'Tin Can'. The hull drummed with the noise of the Perkins P6-65 hp engine, despite efforts to insulate the engine box and wooden cabin roof; it also caused condensation which made it very cold. On 3 June 1951 a Waterloo Pier crew took No. 18 downriver to Wapping workshops for a 300 hours inspection, where the waterside officer there refused to sign for it, having spotted unreported damage to the bows and hull (which might later have been put down to him). So the decision was made to dispose of this persistent ugly duckling. It had completed only 15,531 running hours when, in November 1951, it was put up for sale. The boat that replaced it in January 1952 was mahogany.

Radar was tried during the 1960s but it was not much use. Screens capable

"Forget the fog, he said, I can steer by radar!"
(cartoon by ex-Inspector, Richard Whitworth)

of displaying moored craft, ship buoys, jetties and all the other obstacles to be avoided in bad visibility, were also cluttered with unwanted blips (wave tops and driftwood). Radar had never been needed just because it was dark. Boats' crews found their way about, even on moonless nights, by dint of hard-won local knowledge. Only if caught out in one of London's notorious pea soup fogs, when a man who walked out aft into the sternsheets disappeared from view, were Thamesmen ever lost. Then even the ablest coxswain, convinced he was steering straight, could go in circles. The only safe option was to snatch a quick turn on the first stationary thing you blundered into, and hang on (for hours or even days) until the fog lifted. The Clean Air Acts of 1956 and 1968 eliminated such fogs for good.

Duty boats at speed piled up big following swells. These could result in complaints from small boat users left wallowing and waterlogged astern, or even the occasional threat of an expensive civil claim from a houseboat occupier whose favourite piece of porcelain had fallen over and smashed. It was aggravated up-along where rowing eights and weekend sailors were unused to rough water. Scaled-down duty boats were built and during 1967-8 taken into use patrolling the eighteen non-tidal miles upriver from Teddington Lock to the Metropolitan Police boundary at Staines. These were promptly nicknamed 'Noddy Boats'. They were never ideal and their 40 hp engines could not cope with storm waters flooding down in winter from the countryside.

In January 1975, for the first time in decades, Police bought a different sort of craft. It was a high speed rescue boat, flat-bottomed, made of fibreglass assembled in a tubular frame by Rotorks of Westbury in Wiltshire. The cabin was fitted out with three seats, a locker, lighting, radio, etc. Painted bright orange, with reflective 'POLICE' signs on both sides, it looked like a navvies' hut on a miniature landing craft. This odd vessel, eight metres long, was powered by two Volvo Penta engines of 106 hp each on Z-leg drives, and had a top speed of about 25 knots. Unfortunately, like other radical designs tried by Thames Division, the demands of police work on the tideway defeated it.

The boats are driven hard; yet, pensioned off into private hands, they continue to serve other owners well. Stripped of Police markings and painted grey, they are sold to any broker who submits a successful closed tender. Retired Thames Police boats may be spotted here and there. In the early 1970s there was one at the Thorpe Park amusement complex in Surrey, and two years after the 1982 war, another was working in the Falkland Islands, where her original Perkins P6 engine (dispatched from the factory in 1939 and installed by Osbornes at Littlehampton in 1941) was still pushing it around Port Stanley. The boat had been shipped out during the 1950s, for use by a local food processing plant, and was later purchased by Mr Jack Sollis for general harbour duties and pleasure cruises following a sensible conversion for the shallow inshore waters there. In the mid-1980s local Police patrolled the River Trent and allied Nottingham-shire waterways in a 1952 Osborne boat. It had most of its original fittings, except for a 1974 replacement engine, and was still working every day of the year. One ex-Thames duty boat seen upriver recently at Kingston had been aptly renamed *Off Duty*.

33. The extraordinary flat-bottomed, fast rescue craft by Rotorks of Wiltshire, undergoing trials in 1975.

34. The duty boat Sergeant stands aft and prepares to salute a senior officer aboard the passing 'GreenParrot' launch.

Divisional Chief Superintendent Tom Fallon and Chief Engineer Frank 'Curly' Hodsell (from the Flying Squad) acquired, about 1948, three ex-RAF air-sea rescue launches. Built as seaplane tenders by Thorneycroft, they would replace the *Vigilant*, *Alert* and *Watch* as guv'nors' supervision boats. Each was 40 feet long, with a top speed of about 22 knots made possible by twin Perkins 100 hp diesels, water-cooled, with copper pipes running outside along the bottom of the hull which circulated river water through the engines and back into two header tanks.

These craft arrived in a mess but were soon the smartest launches on the river. Decks and superstructures were restored by the Division's own joiners and carpenters, after which the inside of each cabin was equipped with a table, seats and facilities for making tea and serving snacks to guests. To convert them, a Thames dumb barge (lighter) was obtained for use as a dry dock. When the tide went out the barge ebbed dry and drain valves were opened; then, as the tide returned, the barge filled with water so that a launch could be floated in at one end cut away for the purpose. The barge was pumped dry and made watertight, the launch was chocked up, and both subsequently rose and fell with the tide. This dry dock was kept for subsequent routine services, a useful (if unattractive) feature of the Wapping waterfront for thirty years. The snag was that it rolled and banged about in the wash of passing tugs and ships, making any job uncomfortable for those working inside at the time, while tricky painting had to wait for calmer conditions or when the barge settled on the hard.

The new launches were named *Patrick Colquhoun*, *John Harriott* and *Sir Robert Peel*; but, because of their bright green hulls, they would always be called the 'Green Parrots'. *Patrick Colquhoun* was designated the Commissioner's launch

35. The 40-foot 'Green Parrot' John Harriott, powered by twin Perkins S6 marine diesel engines, heads downriver in 1955.

but most of the time it was used by the Division's chief officer for visits to Stations. Each sub-Divisional senior officer had one for the same purpose. Justified primarily for supervision, State occasions, and as mobile operation control centres for major incidents, these craft were also part of the Force's public relations strategy. They gave trips to members of the Royal Family, senior politicians, other V.I.P.s and celebrities, as well as anyone else who could arrange it.

The Sergeant and two Constables crewing each Green Parrot were generally chosen by seniority and experience. They had to be able to chat easily with Royal or commoner, serve tea and biscuits like first class cabin stewards, and supply a running commentary on the river scene. Relieved of ordinary duties, they cleaned and polished their launches, when not under way, with the diligence of professional deckhands on a rich man's yacht. They were, nevertheless, serving Police officers who, when prompt action was needed, responded if they could do so without endangering their guests.

On one occasion, at least, a Green Parrot itself was in trouble. The *Patrick Colquhoun*, returning late from an evening visit downriver to Erith, dropped the Chief Superintendent off at Wapping and headed home upriver to Waterloo Pier. In King's Reach it hit a submerged object, probably a hefty piece of driftwood, for 'knobblies' (as Thames officers call them) litter the tideway despite the Port of London Authority's best efforts to collect this debris. No harm seemed to have been done. The coxswain came alongside, head into the ebb tide, whereupon his crew skilfully swung the launch (by hand and rope) to lie head downriver in its usual berth. During this manoeuvre the boat was

36. The 1992 renovated command-&-control vessel Patrick Colquhoun (built originally in 1963), in new blue livery, with guests.

sluggish and heavy, and, upon closer examination, the Sergeant found it was making water fast. He re-started the engines, while he still could, and drove back into the upper berth, where the crew slung the boat under the waterside crane to take some of the weight. A duty boat was lashed to the starboard side as extra buoyancy. By the time they had cleared out the long cabin seats and most of the gear, the engines were immersed and the cabin half-flooded. A Fire Brigade boat – the Dunkirk veteran *Massey Shaw* – was called to pump it out. Chief Engineer Fred Byway rushed from home to make and apply a 'tingle' (temporary patch), as whatever hit the hull had found unsuspected wood rot where a metal plate surrounded the toilet discharge pipe. Only then was the launch taken to Wapping and put into the dry dock for repair. It had been a close thing. The launch could have gone to the bottom. Later, apparently, it did. After replacement by a fibreglass boat, the story goes, the *Patrick Colquhoun* was being taken abroad as deck cargo on a ship but was lost overboard in heavy seas.

Fibreglass Green Parrots arrived in 1963. These new craft, with their predecessors names, had twin 144 hp Gardiner engines. They were built by Halmatics on the South Coast and fitted out by Kris Cruisers. Modelled upon the originals, they lacked the finer lines of the wooden boats, with shorter foredecks that made the cabins seem too far forward. Even so, they were splendid craft and younger Thames officers saw nothing wrong with them.

After nearly thirty years, early in 1992, the *Patrick Colquhoun* was sent to

William Osbornes for a major re-fit. It was in good condition for its age. Portions of the cabin and wheelhouse were stripped, as areas around joints and handrails had rotted away. The cabin was lengthened by about five feet and new windows were fitted. The Gardiner engines were replaced with Perkins turbo-charged, 6-cylinder, 3.5 litre, Series 4 engines. This power unit later became standard throughout the Division's fleet. The hull was repainted R.N.L.I. blue, at the instigation of Superintendent Bob Glen, with the name in gold lettering. In return for certain manpower and fleet concessions by the Home Office and the Force Policy Committee, the *John Harriott* was sold. A refit planned to give the *Sir Robert Peel* another ten to fifteen years, pending a replacement, became pointless when it was decided to keep it only until the newly blue *Patrick Colquhoun* was back in use. Then even the *Patrick Colquhoun* was to be sold but, with a policy U-turn, it was retained and converted for use at marine incidents as a command-&-control vessel. Meanwhile, back in the duty boats, Police work was rarely a tea party and could occasionally be perilous.

37. Chief Superintendent Tom Fallon and Frank 'Curly' Hodsell (Chief Engineer) inspect the refurbished Sir Robert Peel on 14 March, 1947.

CHAPTER NINETEEN

Death and Danger

"They are not out for a pleasure trip."
(Master lighterman and jury foreman at the inquest into the death of a
Thames Division Sergeant by drowning, 1913)

It does appear as if everything on the Thames occurs in gentle slow motion.
The river meanders. Boats drift. Ships mooch. But accidents happen in seconds
and the impact forces are always gigantic, as when one nineteenth-century
supervision boat was cut in half by a small but sharp-nosed steamer. The
Inspector, unable to swim, was only saved because he clung to the handle of
an umbrella stretched down to him by a quick-thinking passenger in the bows
of the boat. Comical, as it happened, but the river is always untrustworthy
and often treacherous. Hemmed in by Victorian embankments and quays, the
River Thames is half as wide and twice as fast as it once was. If a boat breaks
down, or is even momentarily out of control, the tide takes charge; and a crew
cannot simply park their craft and walk away, they are swept along with it.
Disciplined skill keeps Thames officers safe for decades at a stretch, just ten
having drowned on duty in a couple of centuries. Misjudge the river however,
or pick up a bad wim-wom, and abruptly it can turn killer.

On a dark Friday evening in January 1913, Sergeant George Spooner with
P.C.s Manktelow and Yates were patrolling the Upper Pool in a motorised
rowing galley. With its 5 hp engine, capable of only five knots in still water,
they barely struggled up through London Bridge. Heading into the strong ebb
tide, which had two hours to run, the skipper reached the upper limit of his
patrol and ferry-glided across the river below Southwark Bridge. He aimed
to pass upstream of moored barges, then turn downriver between them and
the shoreside wharves, checking the security of both as he went. Running close
inshore like this "wiv' the tide up yer arse" (as watermen say) is always risky.
It's like driving a car downhill without brakes – alright only as long as you can
steer round obstacles and do not have to slow down. Stopping is practically
impossible. Then again, approaching the way he did, the turning circle of his
boat was at its largest, except there is a trick to it; entering the slack water at
the downstream end of the last bridge buttress, he poked the boat's bow out
into the tidal stream pouring through the far arch. Spooner had been in the
Division for ten years and would have done this manoeuvre many times under
oars. As the current catches the bow, while the stern is still in slack water, it

In Loving Memory of

GEORGE ERNEST SPOONER,
AGED 34 YEARS.
(late Sergeant, Metropolitan Police ; Thames Division),
WHO WAS DROWNED, JANUARY 10th, 1913.

Interred in Brockley Cemetery.   Grave 1441, Plot K.

38. Sergeant George Spooner, who drowned when he fell from a motorised conversion of a rowing galley that was swept by the tide onto moored barges.

spins a boat in little more than its own length (a bit like a handbrake turn in a rally car). This time it went badly wrong. Somehow, despite the engine going full speed ahead, the boat was carried broadside to end up under the sloping bows of the stationary swim-headed barges. There were oars in the boat but the crew had no time to use them. Fortunately, the boat did not immediately overturn and fill with water; when it did, it could be expected to roll beneath the flat-bottomed craft. Constable Manktelow grabbed hold of the mooring chain, while P.C. Yates scrambled into the barges and then pulled him up too; but George Spooner, when they looked for their Sergeant, had gone, drifting off downstream, encumbered by full uniform and an overcoat. He was seen, still alive, under Cannon Street Bridge but his drowned corpse was recovered days later off Commercial Dock Pier.

At the Rotherhithe inquest it was accepted that Police must go into awkward places and the Coroner commented:

> "Had the engine been strong enough, it seems reasonable to suppose that it would have got him out of trouble. It is a deplorable accident, by which a very valuable member of a very valuable section of the police has lost his life, but perhaps some good will come of it."

The jury returned a verdict of Accidental Death and added:

> "We trust the Commissioner of the Police will soon see his way clear to have the boats fitted with more powerful engines."

Tide tables are, like weather forecasts, only predictions and the river some-times departs from its scheduled ebb and flow. It may one day freakishly not come in, leaving everyone stranded high and dry when they should be on the move; or it may reach the normal high water and go on rising. On 6 and 7 January 1928 a huge flood tide caused havoc. All riverside vaults and cellars were flooded; Wapping's dummy floated free from its moorings; barges were loose all over the place: one sat atop the Shadwell Dock entrance; another had dumped its load of candles (hundreds of tons of them) which littered the surface across to Cherry Garden Pier, mixed up with tarred road blocks lifted and drifted from streets ashore. Tower Bridge was choked with all kinds of flotsam. A ship had broken her moorings and gone athwart King's & Queen's barge roads off Bellamy's Wharf. When eventually the tide fell, a Sun tug at Greenwich buoys found itself resting on top of a sunken lighter. Thames Police crews in their strongly-built but handy teak or mahogany boats were everywhere, with tugmen and watermen, sorting out this mess. One Sergeant drove his boat up Grove Street near Deadman's Dock to help people from their houses (maybe wondering if he should continue to keep to the right, in accordance with the rules of navigation, or to the left as required by the Highway Code).

All the lessons uncomfortably learned in open rowing galleys and the pro-totype motorboats were passed on to each new generation of Thames Police probationers and assiduously practised by them. When, infrequently, they got it wrong, the river could impose a high price for all the trouble-free years, as it did in the early hours of Wednesday morning, 10 November 1937, claiming the lives of two experienced Thames officers. It was just another night duty when Station Police Sergeant Parnacutt paraded his relief (shift) at 9.45 pm at Blackwall. (S.P.S. was a rank – now defunct – between Sergeant and Inspector, which existed only in the Metropolitan Police.)

Frederick William Parnacutt was a character, six foot four inches tall, weigh-ing over twenty stone, with a great appetite for food and amazing strength. Though taciturn and slow of speech, he was no fool. Originally a Ramsgate fisherman, he was studying navigation so that he might have his own boat when he retired. Bill Parnacutt was due to go out 'first four' (10 pm to 2 am) and supervise the patrolling boats, and his section Sergeant was in the process of taking over Station duties, when the S.P.S. changed his mind. He had found some administrative returns due for completion and decided to stay in and do them.

So his Sergeant and crew went out instead. It was a dark and cold night but dry. They had an uneventful run down to Barking, met the Erith boat, and arrived back about 1.45 am for a meal break. "All correct, Sarge," he said to the S.P.S., using the time-honoured Police expression meaning he had nothing to report, for Parnacutt was a man known to go by the book. Then, formalities completed, they both relaxed over their food.

Bill Parnacutt finally went afloat at 2.35 am. When his body was recovered, his watch had stopped at 2.46 am. His crew that last time was P.C. Albert Taylor (who would also die) and P.C. Bob Vincent. Ten minutes after the S.P.S. had cast off, the officers in the Station heard urgent shouting and ran down to the waterside moorings. It came from the crew of the Knights steam tug *Katra*. They had run down and sunk a Police boat. Two men were somewhere in the water; they had a third on board. The tug came alongside with a badly shocked Bob Vincent, who kept repeating to the Sergeant; "Guv'nor, I'm the luckiest man alive." The Sergeant noted that P.C. Vincent's boots were covered with thick mud and concluded that he must have been down on the riverbed with the lost duty boat. He was sent to hospital and a written statement taken from him later read;

> "...off the upper end of Blackwall Police Station, about 100 yards from the North shore, I was standing by the engine with my hand on the water circulating pipe, attending to the engine, when I heard Station Sergeant Parnacutt, who was at the wheel of No. 14 boat with P.C. Taylor sitting alongside him, shout out "Look out Bob, a tug is coming right at us." I looked up and on our port side, amidships, I saw the bows of a tug which was about one yard away and which struck our boat, turning it completely over and the tug went completely over the boat. When I came to the surface I was between the tug and a heavy laden barge."

Every available Police boat was called in to search for the two missing officers. The Harbour Master joined them. At 5 am a Thames Police Inspector spotted the port side of the cabin off Lovell's Wharf, half a mile upriver on the Greenwich side where it had been taken by the flood tide. Later in the day the crew of one of the Harbour Master's launches found the Police boat. They put it ashore at Blackwall where it ebbed dry. The Sergeant's body was still behind the wheel, held there by the steering cable which was drawn tightly over his left shoulder. P.C. Taylor's body was not found until twelve days later. At the inquest at Poplar Coroner's Court, the verdict was Accidental Death. There would not be another drowning in the Division for 28 years.

A year after the loss of No. 14 boat the crew of No. 25 had a narrow escape when it caught fire off Free Trade Wharf, with no warning, and was swept from end to end by flames. At risk every second, they nevertheless delayed long enough to take it out into midriver, clear of laden barges. As they went to jump overboard a waterman, Jock MacFarlane, bravely pulled alongside and took them off; he was rowing them to the Wapping shore when the petrol tank exploded and the Police boat burnt to the waterline and sank.

One young P.C. had the most remarkable experience. Phil Loughe was deckhand in a crew patrolling after an official flood warning of an abnormal spring tide (the highest there is). The water was already at danger level with two more hours to high water. In a dock behind Instones Wharf in Bow Creek lay an odd-looking ship, an American Great Lakes grain carrier which had been loaned to the U.K. during World War II for use as a collier and was now being

restored before returning home. Instead of the usual lock gates, the river was excluded from the dry dock by an *ad hoc* contrivance, a metal pontoon which had been floated into position at low water, so that the pressure of the rising tide plugged it in place. Now the swollen river was lapping at the top, threatening to surmount it, every dirty wave slopping over into the dock basin.

Concerned for the safety of anyone still working in the dry dock, the Inspector and one P.C. landed to have a look. Phil Loughe, the junior crew member, was left to lay off in the boat, head to tide, about six feet away from the pontoon and parallel to it. He was studying the thing when abruptly it reared high into the air and tumbled backwards down into the dock. The river began to pour in after it and the duty boat was carried towards the nascent cataract. The P.C. reacted for his life. He spun the wheel to turn the boat away,

39. The wreck of No. 25 boat, salvaged after catching fire, exploding and sinking on 7 October 1938.

pushing the gear lever to 'Ahead', at the same time opening the throttle. In his urgency he applied power too soon and the engine remained stuck in neutral. The duty boat slipped sideways into the funnelling water.

Keeping his nerve, he shut down the engine revs and pulled the gear lever back into neutral. He tried again. This time he felt the gear slip in and fed the engine full power. It roared like a Spitfire taking off, as he swung the boat's stern around and pointed the bows up and away from the maelstrom; but Phil Loughe could sense he was sliding backwards down into it. The view ahead was restricted to the tilted-up foredeck and the stempost pointing at the sky. He had to turn in his coxswain's seat and look aft over the stern to keep a sense of direction. What he saw was awesome – a tidal wave engulfing the big ship, lifting it up and carrying it bodily to collide with the end wall of the dock. This wave also spilled over and along the dockside, chasing a crowd of fleeing men, his Inspector and fellow P.C. amongst them.

They told him later that, looking back as they ran, they saw the duty boat's propellor turning in the air as the water fell away from it. Now, as the dock rapidly flooded, the water levels equalised, the surface flattened and the screw began to bite. The boat moved forward to safety. Miraculously there were no casualties. Thirteen shore workers ended up soaked but most of the labour force of 300 had been in their canteen at the time. Men in the dock, painting the ship's bottom, had been withdrawn just before the caisson collapsed by an alert manager who did not like the look of it. They entered the hull through an access hole, created earlier by removing plates, and were coming up ladders inside the ship when the wave hit. Even seconds later they would have been battered and drowned. As it was they were merely stranded on the ship's bridge, the only part of the giant vessel left above water.

When the surface settled, Phil Loughe, shrugging off his own shock, took the Police boat into the dock to collect his colleagues. Together they went alongside the sunken ship, recovered the shaken men and arranged for them to be taken home by ambulance. The foundations of the dock, Roman in origin, were irreparably damaged by the flood and it was never used again. There was no such thing as formal stress counselling for policemen in those days, so maybe it was cathartic that P.C. Loughe acquired instant status, despite his short time in Thames Division, to be admired and respected by all with whom he served. From that day in 1947, until he retired as a Sergeant in the 1960s, he was said to be "the only Thamesman who ever drove a Police boat uphill".

40. Salvaging a 'knobbly' (wooden flotsam) that is a hazard to navigation.

CHAPTER TWENTY

Wartime

"...they were called out one night when a Polish seaman on board a merchant ship went berserk and began to fire a Lewis gun... and overpowered the man just as he was in the act of prising the lid off a fresh ammunition box..."
(Chief Superintendent Tom Fallon 1956)

Not a lot is known of the Division's activities during the First World War, since most of the books and files were surrendered and pulped during the Second World War's re-cycling of paper and other scarce materials, although the Roll of Honour lists ten officers killed on active service in the Armed Forces. At the outbreak of that war eight rowing galleys remained but these were restricted to working the upper reaches. The motorised boats downstream had duties which included seizing and guarding any enemy vessels still in the river following the declaration of war, as well as watching for aliens landing, illicit signalling, or carelessness in the screening of lights during air raids. Blackwall boats escorted a great many barges laden with high explosives to and from Woolwich Arsenal. There were civilian casualties and deaths from enemy bombing to be handled, as well as the extra crime which wartime blackouts concealed. Once, when a Thames crew routinely checking a barge heard unexpected sounds of men below, the Sergeant simply closed the heavy hatch, sat on it, and waited for assistance; it turned out they had caught a gang of five, armed with iron bars, who had stolen the barge which contained war munitions valued at £4,000 destined for the French Government.

A German bomb dropped from a Zeppelin airship landed on the foreshore at Winkley's Wharf just below Millwall Dock in 1916. An unladen sailing barge was lying alongside, ebbed dry, and the bomb fell outside of the craft close amidships; it was a puny thing and the barge took most of the blast with little damage. Still, a few windows were broken in a nearby house on the wharf occupied by the manager and his family, and a wharfside brick wall was partially demolished, but nobody was hurt. The anti-aircraft gun across the water at Blackwall Point was a greater hazard, from time to time showering the roof of the Station with shrapnel, bits of which River Policemen's children collected as souvenirs. Officers and their families living in the flats at Blackwall Police Station used the cells as air raid shelters, while residents from the adjacent street, Coldharbour, were allowed into the lower storeroom. The public from further afield on the Isle of Dogs put their trust and their families into Concordia Wharf next door to the Station. This warehouse withstood airborne enemy onslaughts but it would catch alight in 1923 and burn to the ground while packed with raw rubber in plywood chests.

When a train bringing wounded troops home from battle crashed in the old Thames Tunnel, at Wapping underground railway station, the laden stretchers could not be brought out via the steep spiral stairs. Thames Division arrived with ropes and tackles to hoist them up the air shaft to safety.

The Second World War began with an unsettling lack of direct action. In 1939 the ground floor windows at Wapping Police Station were sandbagged and taped to resist bomb blast. The basement was reinforced and an air-raid siren fitted on the roof. Officers were trained in air raid precautions and fire watch duties; neighbourhood air raid shelter instructions were issued in English and Hebrew.

Someone decided duty boats should observe radio silence when enemy aircraft were approaching, so that they could not home in on central London by using radio direction finding equipment. Instead crews, many of whom were already proficient with Morse code, would carry yellow and red semaphore flags; but, as they could only be effective in daylight, when boats in sight of one another could easily come alongside and exchange words, such flag-wagging was of limited use. There are no anecdotes of them ever being purposefully waved by Police – but an Inspector at Wapping reported cautioning a lad for sending indecent messages (to a Police boat?) by semaphore from Horseleydown Stairs. Thames officers had, it was later said, their own unique signalling method. By tucking the corner of an ordinary white handkerchief into the middle button hole of the uniform waistcoat, and then opening and closing it with both hands, line-of-sight messages could be flashed in Morse (at which the radio operators were fluent).

The Admiralty took command over the Port of London and imposed many wartime measures. Names of wharves and warehouses were removed to bemuse spies. Out on the water navigation lights (usually visible for miles) were dimmed to make the task of enemy bombers harder; only private craft with permits could be used; the movement of all vessels was monitored and controlled. Volunteers patrolled from London Bridge to Teddington Lock in private cabin cruisers. One was A.P. (later Sir Alan) Herbert – playwright, composer, lyricist, author and wit – who was a campaigner for women's rights and the Member of Parliament for Oxford University (when it had its own M.P.). Sir Alan lived beside the tideway at Hammersmith, and was acknowledged by Thames watermen, lightermen, sailormen and river police to be a capable riverman, but he received a friendly caution after an excited companion fired the machine gun with which they had been issued at an overhead enemy plane near the Houses of Parliament.

Some 600 Wapping youngsters, women and old people were evacuated to the comparative safety of Richmond, in eight barges towed by tugs, with a Police escort boat ahead to clear the way. The children sang as if it was a day's outing, but for many of the older folk it was their first time away from the East End and they did not want to go. Police had to remove some from their homes, putting them aboard the ferries bound upriver, and they did not appreciate being shipped off like that. "We'll be back," they insisted; and many were, within a few days, preferring to take their chances in familiar surroundings.

World War II – once it got going – was uncomfortable and dangerous for everyone. The first German bombs fell on 7 September 1940, from over 1,000 aircraft, incendiaries that set alight one of the world's biggest stores of timber in the Surrey Commercial Docks. The river was soon covered by choking smoke. Blazing wood and sparks flew through the air, landed on barge tarpaulins and ignited them too. It was a formidable initiation. The smallpox hospital by Commercial Dock Pier evacuated its patients, but the staff became trapped when their escape was cut off to landward, and Police boats ferried the matron and her nurses to safety. There followed 57 consecutive nights of severe bombing raids, which disrupted the docks, shipping and river services, endangering the local dockland communities. Metropolitan Police Commissioner Sir Philip Game boosted morale when, during the worst of the blitz, he chose to travel by water to inspect his Wapping officers and their equipment.

High explosive bombs fell on an old coach-house opposite the Station, blowing in windows of the married quarters, wrecking the boatyard and badly damaging three boats in for repair. In 1941 bombs landing in the river shattered the Station's front windows, put out the lights and flooded moored boats. The following year the Station's blacked-out windows were blown in by near-misses five times in one week.

Lady Basil Henriques was arrested by the Thames officer posted on the front door of Wapping Police Station when he spotted her sketching blast-damaged buildings directly opposite the Station and boatyard. He thought she might be a spy, as drawing and taking photographs were illegal activities, but in fact she had a Government permit to attend the scene of any disaster and record it. Lady Henriques laughed at her adventure and ever after referred to Wapping as "my Police Station". Until shortly before her death she was a familiar figure in the area, continuing in peacetime the drawings which she intended to turn into watercolour paintings.

One Thames officer was killed during the air raids and many had narrow escapes. Parachute mines were a menace. A laden Danish grain ship struck one at Bellamy's Wharf one Saturday at 1.15 pm, the explosion killing two watermen, who were rowing the ship's headrope ashore, also the mate and one or two hands on the fo'c'sle-head at the time. The Navy had minesweepers from Hammersmith Bridge to the Lower Reaches but somehow this one had eluded them. Another time a gang of stevedores, rowing out to discharge a cargo of sugar from a small ship lying at Church Hole Tier, Rotherhithe, were warned off by a Police boat. The officers pointed to the anchor chain where a parachute mine was entangled and sheering about ominously with the tide. They rowed back to the shore, to be shouted at by a Constable standing over by St Mary's Church. He was indicating upwards to where, on a warehouse, another bomb dangled by its parachute cord.

A lot of regular Thames officers, five of whom lost their lives, went off to serve with the Armed Forces. These absent colleagues enjoyed the oddly named *Oggler's Journal,* a duplicated news sheet which kept them up-to-date with home matters, though no mention was allowed of the devastation in the docks or, later, of the flying bombs that fell in London. This newsletter's strange name derives from the nineteenth century when the River Police referred to themselves as 'ogglers', a word probably taken from naval slang word, 'hoggin' or 'oggin', for the sea. Londoners looking down from London Bridge upon the River Police in their rowing galleys (oars like some pond-skimming insect's legs) had called them 'beetles', which is why their modern blazer badge features a water boatman beetle. Officers in the Services were replaced, for the duration of the war, by full-time War Reserves (including divisional pensioners back from retirement) and part-time Special Constables. A typical boat's crew then would be a Sergeant and a Constable, with two Specials.

In 1940 a white letter 'P' was painted on the bows of duty boats as wartime identification, and they were fitted with expanded metal and rubber mesh cabin roof covers to protect them from the shrapnel that could rain down when anti-aircraft batteries were firing upwards. They also had some irregular boats to work with, craft requisitioned from private owners. This was done by Sub-Divisional Inspector Oscar Thompson and Divisional Chief Engineer 'Curly' Hodsell, who together surveyed likely upriver craft. There was a Richardson cruiser, workmanlike (and comfortable), which could be steered from outside as well as inside the cabin. Owners' equipment was carefully removed from the seized boats, itemised, then stored securely at Wapping. Between 1940 and 1942, as new standard pattern duty boats were delivered, the private boats and gear were returned to their rightful owners. None had been lost.

Richmond Lock was targeted by the Luftwaffe, with the object of disrupting barge traffic vital to the British war effort, particularly the transport of petroleum. As well as the usual imports to refineries at the mouth of the Thames, fuel was piped overland from the Severn Estuary to Walton-on-Thames in Surrey, then taken by river to the various oil wharves. A lone German bomber sent on 19 February 1944 achieved one direct hit and another near miss, both of which caused extensive damage. Priority repair work began in June of that year but went on until the end of 1945. The barges were never stopped but could only operate for a few hours around high water. At certain states of tide, with the lock closed, it was impossible for a duty boat to reach the scene of any incident above it; so changeovers took place at Meikles Yard, Twickenham, the crews booking on and off by telephone from Twickenham Police Station. The boats ran down to Barnes for fuel, etc. only when the tides allowed.

P.C. Loughe – who had yet to drive his Police duty boat uphill – came on duty, after a terrifying night of bombs and fires, to be told that his first job was to help take a dead body over to the Rotherhithe foreshore; and then to stretcher

41. Bomb damage to the Wapping boatyard in 1941; the corrugated asbestos roof lies in fragments on the floor and a cabin top is separated from its boat.

it to nearby St Mary's Church where the mortuary had been reopened to relieve others that were packed to capacity. It too was full. From steel scaffolding hung burlap (jute, flax or hemp) bags, each containing a corpse. These were residents from local flats, with their children and babies, and firemen too, all killed in the Surrey Docks conflagration. It was a horrible place, even for trained men, yet the mortuary keeper was a retired waterman assisted by his daughter. He welcomed the officers and proudly showed them a gold watch that had been presented to him at Wapping Police Station. He was Jock MacFarlane who, in 1938, had plucked the crew from their blazing No. 25 boat.

Wapping Police Station was for a time isolated by the blitz. Many local families had moved out; fires were all around, some burning for weeks; bomb damage and general disorder made life primitive. Water had to be brought across the river from Cherry Garden Pier in clean dustbins and the only lavatory was often the foreshore. Single men, and many married officers whose wives and children had been evacuated, slept on makeshift bunks in the Station's reinforced basement. These harrowing days were made cheerful by civilian staff who kept the place as homely as possible. Cooks, canteen assistants and cleaners worked tirelessly (day and night when needed) to provide vital meals and comfort. Friendship, unlike anything in peacetime, made everything bearable. Part of the Station boatyard became a soup kitchen to feed local people made homeless by the bombing. The Station's two elderly female cooks worked valiantly for weeks on a field cooker, every other heat source being out of action. To their aid came an aged woman named Alice. She spent a night sheltering from the bombs, sitting on a bench in the Station cellar clutching her handbag, then decided it was better to busy herself helping others.

Prior to 1940 the only females in the Station were caterers and cleaners. By 1945 Miss Susie Bush and another woman (who lived in the Tower of London where her father was a Yeoman Warder) worked day shifts alongside Police telephonists in the Station office. Between calls they knitted clothing for the troops and clothes for the homeless. Barry Mitchell in the Engineer's Store relied upon Kathy Armstrong, whose older sister Anne was in the boatyard. At least four women toiled in the boatyard: Annie Quarrell, Rosie Rust, Jeannie Gilby and Alice Field cheerfully endured a 44-hour week, with a half day on Saturdays. Under the strict foremanship of a Cornish ex-ship's bosun, Studley Screech, they readied the steamer for the carpenters to bend boat ribs; they caulked, scraped, varnished and painted boats; and they slapped anti-fouling composition on the bottoms of boats; they cleaned out bilges; and they worked the tackle to haul the craft into or out from the boatyard. A female boat cleaner, Mrs. Kathy Robello, did the waterside job. When the war ended these admirable women were gradually absorbed back into peacetime occupations and by 1948 Wapping was almost entirely male again.

CHAPTER TWENTY-ONE

Dragging and Diving

"Once we rescued a Police horse that fell into a canal... Another time we pulled a body from the Regents canal and, when we were changing in our vehicle, a shore based colleague said it was the wrong man. So we went in again...and came across another." (Inspector Phil Johns, 1991)

Beyond the low water reach of nineteenth century mudlarks the river bed was dragged for anything of value by fishermen, using their lines, hooks and nets, from small, manoeuvrable, double-ended Peter boats. Eventually these illiterate but able Petermen did nothing else, working whenever money might be earned, quickly on the scene if a coal barge sank or a ship lost her deck cargo, to salvage all they could. They recovered dead bodies, hoping for a reward but surreptiously emptying the deceased's pockets anyway. A body brought ashore never had cash on it. Gaffer Hexham in Charles Dickens' novel *Our Mutual Friend* admitted as much to his daughter Lizzie, and he knew where to look;

> "Wherever the strong tide met with an impediment, his gaze paused for an instant. At every moving chain and rope, at every stationary boat or barge that split the current into a broad arrowhead, at the offsets of the piers of Southwark Bridge, at the paddles of the river steamboats as they beat the filthy waters, at the floating logs of timber lashed together lying off certain wharves, his shining eyes darted a hungry look."

Petermen might also be paid for giving evidence at inquests – one shilling at Deptford or a munificent five shillings and sixpence at Rotherhithe.

Drowned women float face upwards, old river workers said, but it is not true as a rule. All corpses tend to lie face downwards in the water, with only a rounded back breaking the surface. Of course they do not float at all until decomposition is advanced. A reporter for *The Boy's Own Paper* (c.1884), having viewed official dead body photographs at Wapping, wrote to no doubt awed young male readers (and perhaps their daring sisters too):

> "...no need to ask how this man died – the swollen, sodden, disfigured features indicate too truly the fact of the corpse having been floating up and down the river, lying in the mud, and knocking about among the barges."

42. Divisional shipwrights (1950s) build a flat-bottomed dinghy, with handles to carry and launch it, for use by the mobile dragging unit.

The writer was correct. If not quickly spotted and retrieved, bodies do become bloated and damaged while carried on the flow, hung up on pilings as the tide falls, or entangled with moorings. One young female corpse ('fresh' and otherwise unmarked), I dealt with as a young Thames P.C., had a grotesque flat head because a barge had ebbed dry and sat on it. The Division's officers between them recover 60-80 dead bodies every year. It can be gruesome work, which every crew now and again has to handle, with an increased risk these days of infection.

There were still over one hundred Petermen during Colquhoun and Harriott's time at Wapping and Marine Police boats' crews acquired their skills before they disappeared forever from a changing river scene. Later, when required to recover abandoned weapons or other evidence of crime from the riverbed, Police too knew how to go about it. Eventually Thames Division formed a Mobile Dragging Unit, whereby a spare boat's crew could be posted to a day's search beneath water anywhere in the M.P.D. A special flat-bottomed and broad-beamed dinghy, with gunwale handholds for carrying and launching, was built to be towed on a vehicle trailer to wherever it was needed. In summer this was a pleasant jaunt, enhanced (if the skipper was amenable) by some sunbathing and a beer afterwards; at other times of the year it could be a miserably cold and wet job.

43. An early job for the dragging dinghy in the Serpentine lake, Hyde Park.

Dragging involved blindly trawling the unseen bottom of muddy water with hooks on the ends of ropes or poles, by trailing them over the stern of the boat which was then gently rowed (or allowed to drift with the stream). Hooks of various shapes were tried, some blunt, some sharply barbed, in rows or clusters for different purposes. As they pulled and caught on the bottom, the taut drag line vibrated. Resting a hand upon it, an officer could imagine something of the roughness and debris down below. Some Thamesmen were remarkably successful, akin perhaps to the old-time Petermen who were by reputation sober and steady, persevering, patient, laborious and silent. It was a lot like fishing. Others never had the same feel for it, while the drags too were imperfect implements. Sometimes, when the tide receded and exposed where dragging had been done, whatever was being sought would be found criss-crossed by the marks of the drags which had failed to catch and hold.

At the instigation of Chief Superintendent Tom Fallon during the last war, 'Curly' Hodsell devised an electro-magnetic drag for metal objects. Worked off a battery of heavy accumulators, which barely left room in the dinghy for a crew, it picked up every unwanted bit of scrap iron it touched; but it did recover a gun sought in connection with the mysterious death of a Polish RAF officer found shot on Westminster Bridge. This prototype was so strong that it finally attached itself to a P.L.A. mooring chain, could not be pulled free, and had to be abandoned. Simpler permanent magnets were also tried but they proved to be too weak.

The Metropolitan Police was not the first Force to form a diving unit, although a few officers (including Thames personnel) had suggested it over the years. Credit goes to Berkshire under Chief Constable J.L. (later Sir John) Waldron, C.V.O. It was an immediate success. Essex and other Constabularies soon copied and there are now some 25 units covering the U.K., working on a full or part-time basis, depending upon the workload in each locality.

The Met. watched developments and in 1962 formed its own part-time Underwater Search Unit (U.S.U.) with qualified officers on-call. They also came together once a week to train. Within a year they had so much work that their employment full-time was clearly justified; and in May 1964 – which was when I joined it – the U.S.U. became fully operational from Thames Police H.Q. at Wapping, under Inspector Bob Epps, with his second-in-command Acting-Sergeant (and ex-submariner) Alec Wort.

In the first few years London's U.S.U. responded to about sixty calls a year for assistance from Police divisions. Each job might last a day, or weeks. The rest of the time the divers simply picked a likely spot at random and dived, often surfacing with something that cleared up an entry in a C.I.D. crime book somewhere. Rather than inundate the yards of busy Police Stations with recovered safes, motor bikes, weapons, etc., on which further action might be unlikely, such items were simply logged and left where found. If a query arose later, the Unit knew where to find them again. In this way they learnt what lay on the bottom of every accessible piece of water in the M.P.D. This was how magazine writers and newspaper reporters, assigned to cover Met. Police frogmen in action, always got a good story with pictures. The U.S.U., by picking a familiar spot, could be sure of retrieving an old gun or something. The journalists assumed they were witnessing original finds – and the divers did not disillusion them; or perhaps, shrewder than that, the newshounds were playing the game too.

The Unit's strength is one Inspector, one Sergeant and nine Constables, with a civilian driver, and safety regulations require them to operate with never less than five divers. They work a permanent early turn (7 am to 3 pm), to avoid driving their three tonne van in rush hour traffic, but will turn out anytime and stay late when necessary. The vehicle with its equipment and changing facilities keeps them self-sufficient. With it they also towed on its trailer the old mobile dragging unit dinghy, which proved to be a stable diving boat, before it was replaced by specialised inflatables. Any Metropolitan Police officer hoping to join Thames Division, and this select team, must first serve a probationary period of two years ordinary beat duty in uniform with a land division. It is likely that several more years will elapse before a vacancy occurs and applications are invited. As it happens the Met. has no female diver, although there are some in other U.K. units. In a typical year the U.S.U. now completes some

200 operational searches lasting 264 days. They recover about twenty bodies, twelve firearms, ten edged weapons, fifteen cars and twelve motorbikes, many of these items being clues in an investigation or evidence for a subsequent Court trial.

On-shore police officers faced with a complicated scene of crime call for an expert 'civilian scenes of crime officer' (S.O.C.O. – say "Sock-oh"). It is the S.O.C.O.'s job to handle and preserve exhibits and to transport them to the Metpol's Forensic Science Laboratory at Lambeth. But they do not work underwater. So, until exhibits can be landed, divers must act as S.O.C.O.s too. Merely touching an item may spoil it for the Police scientists, moving it can lose microscopic telltale clues; so, all considered, the U.S.U. does remarkably well. A bank raider fired a shotgun through a protective glass security screen, shattering it and killing a member of staff. The U.S.U. found the gun in the River Thames three months later. So carefully did they handle it that the Police Lab. found 1,150 pieces of glass fragments still on the weapon, over 100 of them in the righthand barrel (which had been fired). This evidence put the gun at the murder scene and other marks placed it in the hands of the accused man who was subsequently convicted. Knives used in stabbings, no matter how long underwater, always provide blood samples. A letter taken from the clothing of a corpse after three weeks immersion yielded fingerprints under laser treatment.

Terrorism is a continual threat to the Metropolis, and the U.S.U. diary fills up months ahead with security searches. For the State Opening of Parliament, an important trial at the Old Bailey, and many other diverse events, the Unit's members will spend days immediately beforehand in sewers, drains, conduits, wells and reservoirs under the streets and buildings, looking for bombs and

44. The Underwater Search Unit locates and retrieves a murder weapon.

45. Squelching about in a sewer is best done in a diving suit.

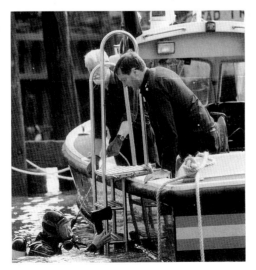

explosives. The day after an I.R.A. explosion killed two people and destroyed buildings at South Quay in West India Dock, the divers went to work. During ten days of 12-hour shifts, in almost nil visibility, they negotiated decades of sunken debris (plus three abandoned cars), overlaid with a fresh carpet of shattered glass, to locate and retrieve invaluable forensic fragments of twisted metal from the bomb blast.

Dead bodies found underwater are usually still fresh; so the search fee earned by Thames boat crews, who handled floaters in an advanced state of decomposition, is never claimed by U.S.U. divers. However, groping about in the dark for a body – and coming across it by putting your hand in its mouth (as I once did) – still requires steady nerves. They also assist when exceptionally high tides look like flooding London; they liaise with Customs & Excise (who have no divers of their own), searching the outside of ships' hulls for contraband attached below the waterline; and defray the cost to tax payers with D.I.Y. repair work to Police boats and riverside premises in any spare duty time. What few hours remain each year fill up with administration, court appearances, training and leave. All the divers have attended confined space search courses, and are equipped with lightweight breathing apparatus (including mini gas analysers), so as to cope with an increasing number of calls to toxic gas escapes in both boats and buildings .

There is no really deep water in London. A few reservoirs or gravel pits go down 15-20 metres but most are half that depth. Although their equipment will function down to around 50 metres, much of a Met. U.S.U. diver's work is done in shallow lakes, gravel pits, ponds, streams, ditches and canals, as well as water cisterns atop blocks of flats or offices. Even crawling over boggy ground is best done in a diving suit. If it is damp, a Police diver has probably been there.

Even simple tasks become tricky underwater. Imagine you are given some bits of wood, nails and a hammer, and told to sit in the deep end of your local swimming pool and construct a box. The wood floats, the nails sink and the water smothers your efforts with the hammer. Another example. Fit a spanner to a tight nut and bolt and pull. The nut will not shift but you will go drifting off at a tangent if you do not anchor yourself somehow. It is like being a weightless astronaut, except that astronauts can see. There are no snapshots of the U.S.U. at work beneath the surface. Unlike divers in tropical holiday advertisements, they do most of their work in nil, or extremely poor, visibility, finding their way by touch, with search lines laid out in grid or circular patterns. It requires great self-reliance as Police divers work alone; in pairs, one would never know where exactly the other one was, which could prove hazardous to both. They often rely upon surface-demand air supplies, because they cannot see to read the contents gauge on the air bottle of self-contained underwater breathing apparatus. A diver must be careful not to tangle his or her airhose and lifeline, so, to avoid a dangerous snarl up, turns to left and right must be alternated. Diving is a slow and methodical procedure which takes training.

The Police Service has two diving schools and every Police diver goes to one or other of them. One is at Strathclyde but Metpol officers use the National Diving & Marine School at Sunderland which was established in 1976 and is run by the Northumbria Police. The basic residential course there lasts two months, with practice dives in the docks and sea, where divers learn search techniques and salvage work such as raising safes by means of air bags. After two or three years working with their own units divers return to school for a two week refresher course. With four or five years under his or her weight-belt an officer may qualify as a supervisor, with a refresher course two to five years after that. So, although a new diver should become a useful team member after only a few months, it takes up to ten years to master the trade. Divers may stay with the Unit, subject to continued aptitude and fitness (compulsory annual medicals last two days), until they retire from the Police on age limit at 55 years old or more.

The Unit now uses a variety of makes of diving gear; members who are certificated by the manufacturers maintain this in the Unit's workshop at Wapping. Diving, like other potentially dangerous pursuits, is made safe by a combination of training, tests, law, experience and strict discipline. Errors and oversights, or unforeseeable bad luck, can be fatal. In the twenty years that U.S.U.s have existed in the U.K. six Police divers have died. No operational Metpol diver has lost his life but, on 15 February 1989, Constable Mark Peers fell victim to an unsuspected medical condition and died undergoing a candidate's diving aptitude test.

The U.S.U. has transformed underwater searches for clues and evidence. A suspect hoping to thwart investigators could, years ago, say (of loot, a weapon or whatever); "I threw it into the river. You'll never find it." And men of the old dragging unit, if unsuccessful in a search, could only say to an investigating officer: "We can't find anything." Police divers can now state; "It isn't there." Detectives can then return to suspects and say with certainty; "No you didn't. Now tell us what you really did with it."

Although recent cuts and reorganisation within Thames Division left the U.S.U. untouched, consideration is being given to whether or not it remains economical for each individual Constabulary to maintain its own diving unit. If not, then mergers and agency agreements become the likely future of policing underwater.

CHAPTER TWENTY-TWO

Further, Faster

"Below, on the river itself, a police launch patrolled the polluted waters, its engine thudding rhythmically against the tide."

(Michael Shea, Author, 1982)

From the upper deck of a red London bus beside the river you may spot one of Thames Division's latest black and white duty boats. They seem small but are actually as long and wide and powerful as the bus. It is the river, a quarter of a mile across even in town, which dwarfs them.

The Police boat is a thoroughbred. Over several generations bad features have been ruthlessly eliminated to fit it for Police work. It is fast, racing along in an emergency, with the sharp stem cutting the water while the flared bows lift to river swells. Strong (as much tug as speedboat), with a large propellor deep in the water, it can pull vessels several times its own size. A strong towing post amidships was essential when laden lighters often came adrift from barge roads; but broken-down private craft, which are smaller and less of a burden, can be handled from a stirrup between strong mooring dollies on the quarters of a twin-screw launch. The forward steering position, impractical for sea-going craft, aids precise boat handling, the large cabin windows giving all-round visibility. Steering must also be responsive going astern, never an easy manoeuvre. At cruising speed the engine has to be quiet and vibration-free, so that the crew can hear their radios and be comfortable for hours at a stretch.

A curved forefoot and strong keel enable boats to be driven onto the hard if necessary. Coxswains may also risk touching bottom when they cut corners ('short-shoring'), sneaking into slack water to cheat an adverse tide and make good time on a long run. Underwater aft, a skeg protects the propellor and shaft of single-screw boats from foul bottoms; but skegs spoil the performance of twin-engined boats which do not have them. The low cabin top enables a boat to be taken where there is limited headroom under jetties and gangways. Searchlight, radio aerial, mast, navigation lights and horn are never too firmly fixed, since Police coxswains have been known – when delay could cost lives – to open the throttle and knock the lot off on overhead obstructions. Freeboard is a compromise. It must keep out the short, steep waves that typically slop about the Thames tideway; while waist and sternsheets have to be low enough for officers leaning outboard, without overbalancing, to reach bodies (living or

46. No. 11 glass fibre Patrol Boat, P6 marine engine, in 1958.

dead) in the water. The flat after-deck can accommodate casualties being resuscitated and stretcher cases.

The post-War fleet worked well for twenty years. Then fibreglass ousted wood. A moulded Police patrol boat was introduced to the Division in 1958, built by Watercraft, fitted out by Tough Bros. of Teddington. No. 11 boat followed, powered by the standard Perkins 65 hp diesel engine, with a speed of 12 or 13 knots. The cabin still had no doors and (like all the others) allowed the deckhand to become drenched in driving rain with a following wind. Half-height canvas dodgers gave only partial protection. A sectional drawing of the boat was featured as a centre-fold illustration in the *Eagle* comic in November the same year. Ten years later the Division's thirty boats were all glassfibre 30-footers, with single Perkins 105 hp diesels capable of 14-16 knots at 2,000 revs per minute. Each one had cabin doors and Thames officers at last could discard their tilts and woolly boat coats in exchange for light-weight protective garments.

Then in February 1976, the Division went shopping yet again for new boats, as the average age of the fibreglass ones was twelve years (and No. 11 was eighteen years old). They chose TaskForce Boats Ltd. model TF9 15/30 for the replacement duty boats (R.D.B.s) and the job of building them was sub-contracted to Mustang Marine at Cowes on the Isle of Wight. The TF9 was the metric equivalent of existing duty boats; length overall 9.14 m; beam 2.74 m; draught 0.84 m. It was an easy riding and stable craft which handled well. The cabin interior had ample workspace, clear headroom, sensible seats and

"Ready to go afloat – got your high visibility anorak, high bib overtrousers, welly boots, body suit, gloves, woolly pully, self inflating lifejacket, epaulettes, truncheon, pocket books, knife, sunglasses, clipboard, beret, scarf, grub, portable marine radio, PFX and vodafone?"
(cartoon by ex-Inspector Richard Whitworth)

all-round vision. The tried and trusted Perkins T6:354(M) 220 hp six-cylinder engine, within its soundproofed engine box (sturdy enough to jump down onto from a ship under way) gave a maximum speed of twenty knots at 2,600 rpm. and an economical patrol speed of fifteen knots. Fuel tanks of 150 gallons capacity were built into the hull. Economic running combined with low wash at speed. It was made for Police duties.

The wooden towing post amidships, permanently rigged for use, was one feature of the old boats to be retained, along with a solid keel and skeg. Innovations included a weed hatch, to reach propellor and prop-shaft from the stern deck. This went largely unused, since Thames wim-woms defy ineffectual fiddling at arm's length. Thames officers are rightly suspicious of untried gimmicks; when one boat was started up with the hatch still open, the spinning propellor quickly flooded the sternsheets. They imagined what might happen if it accidentally turned over while one of them was working on it. A foredeck hatch now housed the anchor, removing the chance of a giant swell washing it overboard on the end of its chain – which had happened occasionally. A neat console incorporated both Force and Marine radios. The bilge pump was versatile; it could empty the duty boat, or another craft, and (hoses reversed) it would fight fires. By the mid-1980s Thames Division had seven of these R.D.B.s.

At about the same time in 1977, with the closure of Stations on Blackwall and Barnes Sub-Divisions, it became imperative to go even further and faster.

Single-screw duty boats took from one to two hours, noisily flat out from Wapping, merely to reach Erith. If they were delayed by actual Police work along the way, patrols went uncompleted. Useful response to an emergency call below Crayford Ness, from the Essex or Kent Constabularies or the P.L.A. would only be possible if patrols ranged greater distances from base. So another change was begun, this time to 34-foot, long-range, twin-screw fast patrol boats.

Chief Superintendent D. Hunt and Fred Byway drafted the specification for these boats with 9 feet 3 inches beam and 3 feet draught. A one-piece fibreglass hull (previous boats had hulls made in two halves split along the midline) would have cabin and decks secured with stainless steel bolts covered by glassfibre. Precursors emerged from the mould at the Tyler Boat Company, Tonbridge, Kent, in 1978, and were transported by road to Porter & Haylett at Wroxham in Norfolk to be fitted out and the decks covered with Treadmaster. Subsequent hulls went to Tough Bros. at Teddington for final fittings. Powered initially by twin 250 hp Sabre six-cylinder turbo-charged engines, speed trials over a measured mile at Great Yarmouth in September 1976 revealed a speed of 28 knots. They had a range of 150 miles at fifteen knots. Both engines had intercooled, direct injection, transmission K.G. 506 twin disc gearboxes, handed 19 x 28 N.A.B. propellors, steering Morse control, and stainless-steel prefabricated rudders filled with mineral oil.

The original Sabre engines suffered from the harsh demands made upon them – all that charging about on emergency calls, often from a cold start – and had to be replaced. The Division returned again to Perkins for their turbo-charged 3.5 litre Series 4 (subsequently Perkins/Sabre) six-cylinder marine engines. A single unit drove the smaller R.D.B.s, while twin engines powered fast patrol boats and the guv'nors' launches. This meant the engineers had to stock only one range of spares and tools, while engines from out-of-service boats could be cannibalised for parts.

These big long-range boats had aluminium sliding doors. A comrehensive dash panel was fitted with Morse Teleflex controls. Other equipment included a magnetic compass, loudhailer and Seafarer echo-sounder, and there was an efficient cabin heater. Forward, through the wheelhouse, a galley was fitted with a stove and sink unit, toilet and locker for coats. All bulkheads were lined with formica for easy cleaning. The addition of V.H.F. sailor radios to the twin-engined fast patrol boats (and to R.D.B.s) was welcomed by Thames officers as, for the first time in their history, they could now hear, and talk with, the ships, tugs and watermen on the move around them.

Any different kind of high speed rescue-and-response boats the Division may buy in future are likely to be rigid inflatables. Some have been tried. They have high speeds, remarkable manoeuvrability and negligible wash. Stability is sometimes uncertain, however, while one boat's propellor had to be replaced after only five days due to damage from 'knobblies'. Jet drives may seem the obvious alternative but these have yet to survive trials and at least one proved to be useless going astern. Having compromised in the past with boat design,

47. Overt and covert peace-keeping; a long-range fast patrol boat in Lambeth Reach passes the M.I.5 building below Vauxhall Bridge.

only to regret it later, the Division has no intention of doing so again. The Engineer's Department early in 1992 specified 35 knots sustainable for three hours; they remain optimistic that some builder will produce their ideal craft and other private fleet owners keenly await the outcome. The first long-range fast patrol boat was transported by road to Boatex at Woolwich, lifted into the water, and brought the final few miles to Wapping by river. As it rounded the point at full speed, many officers sensed unsettling new times approaching.

CHAPTER TWENTY-THREE

Then....

"There was one man at the rudder, one to tend the engines, and two burly police-inspectors forward... our craft was evidently a very fast one."
(Arthur Conan Doyle, Author, 1889)

As January yielded to February 1814, mini-Ice Age weather froze the Thames solid. Watermen, deprived of their usual living, charged two shillings and threepence admission to citizens venturing onto the ice for what turned out to be the last great Frost Fair. The various amusements included archery, horse racing, jesters and jugglers; and rides in the watermen's own (stranded) horse-drawn wherries. There were souvenir sellers, food and drink tents, as well as satisfaction for lewder appetites. A token penny was demanded to go ashore again, although this had often to be waived for those totally spent – in every way – from their revelries on the ice. Some watermen pocketed an ordinary week's takings in a single day.

No doubt Marine Police Surveyors and their men patrolled the fair on foot. For, crime aside, it was a risky venture. Near Blackfriars Bridge a plumber named Davis, taking a short-cut from one side of the river to the other with a load of lead, fell between two ice masses and was drowned. Two young women were rescued from a similar fate by a couple of watermen. A week later, as the thaw set in, a pair of well-dressed young men were also drowned when an ice floe on which they were marooned, shouting for help, tipped them into the river. When new embankments confined the river, it flowed faster; and these, combined with an increasingly milder climate, put an end to Frost Fairs.

Joseph (later Sir Joseph) Bazalgette, Chief Engineer to Victorian London's Board of Works, designed and in 1865 completed the capital's sewer system, reducing river stink and diseases. Then, between 1862 and 1874, he built the Victoria and Chelsea embankments, using granite quarried from Cornwall, Dartmoor, Lundy Island, County Wexford and Brittany in France. In the process Bazalgette eliminated most of the old draw docks, slipways, holes and stairs which had provided easy access to and from the waterside. Fewer landing places, a long way apart, still make problems for the emergency services today.

River crossing points, however, increased. The only one that had concerned Colquhoun and Harriott was the ancient London Bridge, with its twenty irregular pointed stone arches, which had obstructed the Thames since at least 1209.

As patrols reached further upstream, however, they had to contend with other newer structures: Blackfriars (1769); Westminster the first in the centre of the capital after London Bridge (1750); Battersea (1772) whose nineteen timber spans featured in more than one Whistler painting; Putney, with eighteen wooden buttresses, designed by Dr. William Cheselden, a surgeon at St. Thomas's Hospital (1729); Kew's stone King George III bridge (1789), which had replaced an 11-span wooden affair with a toll gate, owned by the enterprising Tunstall family who previously operated a horse ferry there; and Richmond (1777).

Every one of the 29 Thames bridges eventually built contributed to river accidents and suicides. Hopeless souls jumped off them. Scaffolding collapsed, dumping workmen into the river's muddy rush. Ships collided with – or became grindingly stuck beneath – them. From Blackfriars Road Bridge downstream to London Bridge, there were five bridges in a mere six-tenths of a mile. To line up a way through this obstacle course of overlapping arches, all of different sizes, required unerring judgement from any ship's pilot. Unladen 'flat-iron' colliers on the move – each the size of an office block – could only make the downriver trip (and maintain steerage way) punching into a rising flood tide. They had little headroom to start with, and not much time to clear them all. If in doubt, full speed ahead was rung, since any hesitation saw the water level rise, one foot every fifteen minutes, and shipowners viewed with disfavour a master who missed the tide. No wonder these monsters from time to time became wedged within bridge holes.

Vauxhall (originally named Regent's) Bridge was the first cast iron Thames bridge (1816). The Strand Bridge, when its cornerstone was laid (in 1811), became Waterloo Bridge (1817) after Wellington's celebrated victory. Southwark (1819) was the largest cast iron structure then built. Hammersmith (1827) was the first Thames suspension bridge, with Brunel's Hungerford (1845) for pedestrians after it. Others were Richmond and Barnes Railway Bridges (1848 & 1849), Chelsea Suspension Bridge (1858) and Grosvenor (or Victoria) Rail Bridge (1860) taking trains of the London, Brighton & South Coast Railway.

The foundations of Westminster Bridge were scoured out and undermined by the faster flow that resulted from Rennie's new London Bridge (1831) and a replacement (1862) had to be built. Tides now reached Teddington, which became barely navigable at low water. Teddington Lock was bridged (1889); and a half-tide weir, lock and bridge were constructed at Richmond (1894). Lambeth suspension bridge (1862) replaced an ancient horse ferry. Battersea (1863) was jointly owned by the London & North Western and the Great Western Railway Companies.

When Charing Cross Railway Bridge (1864) replaced the old Hungerford Bridge, Brunel took the secondhand chains to complete his Clifton Suspension Bridge at Bristol. Blackfriars Rail Bridge, for the London, Chatham & Dover Railway, used stones from the demolished Westminster Bridge. Cannon Street (1866) is actually Alexandra Bridge. Tower Bridge (1894), state-of-the-art Victorian engineering, stone-clad as a fanciful Gothic castle, was the first crossing downstream of London Bridge. Then, as part of the upriver Great Chertsey Road building scheme came Chiswick, Hampton Court and Twickenham (all 1933).

Only a few of these bridges confronted Lieutenant Peter Halkett, R.N. on 10 June 1844 when he completed, with two companions, the first recorded trip in a rubber dinghy down the Thames from Kew to Westminster Bridge. His vessel was one of those eccentric Victorian inventions. Made by him from indiarubber cloth, it really could be worn as a cloak until needed as a boat; then it was puffed up with bellows. The boat later won an exhibition prize medal, was manufactured, and some were certainly used by expeditions. It was the forerunner of modern inflatables. The Lieutenant had a sense of humour, his handwritten 'Log of the Good Ship Boat-Cloak' recording; "...grog almost expended... ship's company in low spirits... symptoms of mutiny on boat (his friends wanted to land and visit a pub)... captain claps both gentlemen in irons." He also remarked upon "...a first-rate looking building newly erected on the shore," which was the latterday House of Commons, the previous Palace of Westminster having burnt down ten years earlier.

In his melodrama *The Sign of Four*, Conan Doyle tells how Sherlock Holmes and Dr. Watson board a River Police launch at Westminster Pier and make their way to the Pool of London, "...shooting the long series of bridges which span the Thames." What follows is the first fictional account of a powered boat chase:

> "The furnaces roared, and the powerful engines whizzed and clanked like a great metallic heart. Her sharp, steep prow cut through the still river-water and sent two rolling waves to right and to left of us. With every throb of the engines we sprang and quivered like a living thing. One great yellow lantern in our bows threw a long, flickering funnel of light in front of us. 'Pile it on, men, pile it on!' cried Holmes, looking down into the engine room...'Get every pound of steam you can.' "

So they pursued the dainty, fast steam launch *Aurora* downriver – past the West India Docks and along Limehouse Reach to Greenwich; turned northwards around the great bight of the Isle of Dogs to Blackwall; went eastwards again down Bugsby's Reach, Woolwich Reach, to Gallions and Barking Reaches, off the Plumstead Marshes. There those two worthy Victorian gentlemen shot dead Tonga, the grotesque black dwarf with his poison darts and murderous blowpipe, taking alive his not unlikeable white employer Jonathan Small. Stereotypically flawed these days, it remains Thames Division's foremost literary outing.

River Police have perambulated London's longest highway throughout the reigns of nine Monarchs, from George III to Elizabeth II, always with a role in pomp and circumstance occasions. In 1849 Prince Albert rode, standards flying, in a seventeenth-century royal shallop with gilded canopy, propelled by eighteen liveried oarsmen, to open the new Coal Exchange at Billingsgate. The same barge was used by George V and Queen Mary for the peace pageant of 1919. In 1945, as part of the victory celebrations for the ending of World

48. *Icicles on the engine box – a cold tour of duty in the winter of 1947.*

49. *......and a wet one in 1948.*

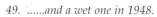

50. Above Richmond in the 1960s, giving a cautionary word to young bathers.

War II, George VI (with the King of Norway and Marshall Tito) rode afloat from Southend to Parliament Buildings; and, on 8 June 1946, the King and Queen, with the Princesses Elizabeth and Margaret, joined a river procession in the Royal Barge, their progress spearheaded by five Thames Division boats.

The Marine Police must have been part of the flotilla of small craft which accompanied Lord Nelson's coffin on its way by river from lying in state at Greenwich to St Paul's Cathedral for his funeral in 1806. No doubt too, then as Thames Division, they watched the Lord Mayors' Shows, colourful water pageants, until the City of London surrendered control of the Thames to its new Conservators; although one more was held – in 1953 – as a 500th anniversary celebration to coincide with the coronation of Elizabeth II, a 3-mile procession of 150 craft from Greenwich to Westminster. Thames officers saw many of the 'little ships' hurrying downriver to join a cross-Channel armada for the typically British pro-amateur evacuation in 1940 of our trapped troops from the beaches of Dunkirk. Sir Winston Churchill's funeral cortege in 1965 was also waterborne.

The Oxford and Cambridge boat race was from 1836-64 held, prior to its present course, in central London from Westminster Bridge upriver to Putney. Thames officers were at the start of Captain Matthew Webb's 18-mile swim downriver in 1875 from Blackwall to Gravesend, five hours of leisurely breast stroke with the ebb-tide, a publicity stunt before his epochal Channel crossing, for which he collected on a £10 bet at two-to-one odds. Between 1877 and 1892 they safeguarded a Lords & Commons race swum over various five to six mile courses between Charing Cross and Kew. Then, on 14 June 1980, British journalist and super-marathoneer Kevin Murphy entered the River Thames at Richmond in Surrey and swam his powerful crawl stroke down over the ebb. Meeting the flood in the vicinity of the Woolwich Thames Barrier, he stemmed

51. *Jimmy (later Sir Jimmy) Savile, through his TV programme 'Jim'll Fix It', arranged for Wendy O'Brien to launch a Thames Police boat.*

52. *Commemorative plate affixed to motor boat Wendy.*

M. V. 8. "WENDY"

WAS LAUNCHED BY MISS WENDY O'BRIEN
AT SHORHAM ON 20/11/68
FOR SERVICE WITH THE METROPOLITAN POLICE.

CONSTRUCTED BY
WATERCRAFT (SHOREHAM) LTD
No. 1297
1968

the tide (swimming non-stop) for five hours or so, then rode a second ebb to emerge about forty miles and 18 hours later at Gravesend in Kent.

In April 1884 an editorial in the *Richmond & Twickenham Times* complained of drunken and loutish behaviour by river ruffians who, in the absence of Police, vandalised riverside property and boats ... and bathed indecently. The solution, those consulted all agreed, was to further extend Thames Division's jurisdiction and patrols upriver from Battersea Bridge to (say) Teddington. The Commissioner's response was a penny-pinching compromise; volunteers from 'T' and 'V' shore divisions would patrol in rowing boats on their rest days, only at weekends and Bank Holidays during the summer boating season. Constables performing this extra duty would be paid an allowance of five shillings a week (Sergeants, six shillings). Those officers must have had some balmy days out on the river at the taxpayers' expense and Jerome K. Jerome's *Three Men in a Boat* might well have come across them, although he does not mention it. Anyway, the patrols were useless; rowdyism and crime went unchecked.

A report by Thames Police Superintendent Chisholm in July 1893 pressed for an increase in men and boats to work upriver; and the following year Union Lighterage was just one of many barge firms complaining of pilferage from craft – in their case at Hammersmith Dock – who backed him up. That same year the steam launch *Henderson* was acquired, with moorings at Barnes and facilities in the nearby Police Station for the crew, whose job it would be to supervise the existing 'land crab' rowing patrols. Eventually Thames Inspectors (3rd class) and eight P.C.s replaced the 'T' & 'V' Division officers, although in 1907 the *Henderson* was issued a lock pass to keep an eye on the sole rowing patrol still active upstream. Motor launches *Howard*, *Lady Henry* (the *Henderson's* replacement) and *Helen Henry* also had lock passes in 1909.

It was the practice, before Peel's Police, for Justices of the Peace to call upon irregular Special Constables whenever they had reason to expect any tumult, felony or riot. An Act of Parliament passed in 1831 amended the law relating to them and it is the source of today's Metropolitan Special Constabulary. In 1935 the Home Office established a river section of the M.S.C., which has continued to assist the regular officers for over sixty years. In 1983 the first woman Special appeared afloat, not long after the first regular female Thames officer, P.C. Anne Hunt.

On 10 September 1949 there was a Review of the Thames River Police by H.M. Secretary of State for the Home Department, The Rt. Hon. Chuter Ede, M.P. to mark the 150th anniversary of their establishment. A river pageant proceeded from Greenwich to the Palace of Westminster. The souvenir programme for this event recalled how in 1797 losses on the Thames totalled £506,000 and estimated the loss for 1947 at exactly £2,003 10s 2½d.

From 1902 many letters had complained of riverside crime at Hampton Wick. Despite many reports written by officers in the intervening decades, it would be over sixty years before a pilot scheme for policing this upriver section was carried out. Then on 4 April 1966 a new Thames Police Station appeared at

53. Rescuing swans with oily plumage.

54. Somewhat bedraggled, birds and officers alike.

55. *Sculling against the flood tide to collect a boat from Waterloo Pier's mooring buoys upriver from the Royal Research Ship, Discovery.*

56. *A pageant and review of Thames Division in a choppy King's Reach, on 10 September 1949, to commemorate 150 years of river policing.*

57. Sally the seal, rescued by Thames police in July 1962, awaits her return to the sea by the R.S.P.C.A.

58. P.C. Anne Hunt, the first female Thames police officer, climbs a ship jetty ladder at low water in 1983.

Shepperton, with Police moorings above and below the lock to eliminate the lengthy process of locking through; and, in 1967, Hampton Station was opened on the river island known as Platts Eyot (pronounced 'eight' and sometimes spelt 'ait').

By the mid-1970s the Division operated a fleet of 33 motor boats from seven Stations with a total of 216 officers. It was the strongest they would ever be. At about this time a retired lighterman, Jack West, worked as a Police boat cleaner at Wapping. He was a respected Freeman of the River who, in his final year as a young apprentice, had won the prestigious Doggett's Coat-and-Badge sculling race. Asked by Inspector Ron Turner to say, honestly, how rivermen felt about Thames Division, the loyal 73-year-old replied; "They luvs yer, boy; they luvs yer."

CHAPTER TWENTY-FOUR

. . . . And Now

"There is valuable work to be done – and it is being done by night and day, by the men who man the dark launches which can swoop dramatically, or nose quietly, into the quiet corners of the tideway."

(Glyn Hardwicke, author, *c*.1985)

Combative labour relations in the 1970s caused traditional cargo ships to stay away and this helped to ruin London's docks. New load-on-load-off container vessels then made the dockers redundant and the move to deeper water on the east coast made the buildings irrelevant as well. With no cargoes to shift, lightermen too were laid off, their barges broken up and sold for scrap metal. Remaining tugs-and-tows are few; wharves lie derelict; cranes rust, unused. Some warehouses have been demolished and replaced with imaginative new buildings; others are now converted into expensive flats, trendy pubs, estate agents' offices and at least one fitness studio.

The Division, too, is drastically changed. Its strength has in recent years been halved. By April 1995 the establishment was down to 137 officers: one Superintendent; one Chief Inspector; six Inspectors; 22 Sergeants; and 107 Constables. The fleet consists of just six twin-screw fast patrol boats (the seventh was written off when it hit driftwood and then veered out of control to smash into an unyielding moored barge), twelve replacement duty boats, two rigid inflatables and the *Patrick Colquhoun* as the Divisional Command Vessel. Each patrol boat runs for 2,500 hours a year and, as the fleet consumes 75,000 gallons of diesel, three boats were moth-balled for a while to save their running costs. Budget cutbacks make it necessary to keep and refurbish these ageing boats when they might otherwise be replaced.

Hampton Station was the first to be shut down, on 1 July 1978, when it was redesignated as a mere mooring. Erith suffered the same demotion on 1 November that year; Barnes was next (1 January 1979), and then Blackwall on 1 September the same year. Twelve years later, on 15 August 1991, Waterloo Pier (central London's landmark floating Station) also closed; and on 14 October night patrols ceased on Barnes Sub-Division. Shepperton was closed in 1992 and Barnes too was subsequently shut down. Also in 1992, as a result of a new scheme called Sector Policing, it was decreed that all H.Q. branches – including Thames Division – should lose 15% of their establishments, which for them meant fifteen officers. A few were able to return as civilians with such titles as Fleet Officer, Local Intelligence Officer and Stores Liaison Officer. Before this tidal wave of change had spent itself, however, a reformation had begun.

In 1989 a review of the Division's methods for dealing with dead bodies revealed that, in the preceding forty years, about a hundred corpses taken from the Thames had been buried unidentified – at the local authorities' expense – without relatives having been traced. This was about one out of every twenty recovered.   A Divisional Investigation Officer (D.I.O.) was appointed, taking over duties previously done by the C.I.D. with the assistance of uniformed officers in each individual case.   The D.I.O. is a Thames Division officer, responsible for all matters relating to dead bodies recovered from the Thames below the high water mark between Dartford Creek and Staines Bridge, as well as all other directly accessible and navigable waterways. Suspicious deaths still involve the C.I.D; otherwise the D.I.O. investigates the circumstances of death, prepares and presents evidence at Coroners' Courts, and is uniquely expert on such matters. The diseases associated with dead bodies are hepatitis, HIV and leptospirosis, all of which may be contracted by the transfer of fluids through open wounds, eyes, nose and mouth. As a consequence, officers handling river corpses now routinely wear protective clothing, including (if necessary) face masks with plastic goggles.   All such garments and gear are subsequently disposed of as contaminated waste; and any area in which a body has been placed must be decontaminated.

Until the 1970s P.C.s joined Thames Division early in their careers and remained in it, with or without promotion, until they retired. Apart from some classroom tuition during their probationary six months, on-the-job training was unspecified and haphazard, but lengthy and generally thorough. After several years most men were accomplished boat-handlers able to cope afloat with anything they might be called to do. It is different now. Officers are encouraged to move from one part of the Service to another, eliminating career specialisation. A five-year maximum posting has been mooted for Thames Division, although it has yet to be implemented, but promotion within the Division is no longer possible.   Inspectors and Sergeants arrive with no previous river experience. Training must be structured and concentrated, so in 1990 a Divisional Training Unit was established.

Newcomers learn all sorts of fresh skills: boat handling theory and practice; radio procedures; marine law; waterborne diseases; what to do with a dead body from the river. Each year at least two basic boat courses lasting five weeks are held, as well as some sailing instruction in the Division's own dinghy, which is an ex-Admiralty 16-foot pull-and-sail boat (nostalgically named *Antelope* after one of the Marine Police cutters). Every successful recruit is awarded a certificate and issued with a personal training log book. At six months, officers progress to a three week course which focuses on the navigation and pilotage required for the Department of Transport Boatman's Licence. At eight months there is a further three week advanced boat handling course. Using the goodwill and cooperation of local contacts, it is possible for officers to take the helm of a yacht, river bus, hovercraft, pleasure boat, tug and ship. After all, they may at any time be called to board and take charge of one. This dynamic individual development now includes Royal Yacht Association (R.Y.A.) courses – endorsed 'Commercial' – for Day Skipper and Yachtmaster certificates. Boat handling is also, increasingly, about high-speed rigid inflatable skills.

"Sit down, shut up and get your hair cut" instructors (if they ever existed) have gone for good. Emphasis is now placed upon individual responsibility for personal development by means of open-access computerised learning. Self-teaching programmes, available 24 hours a day, also enable officers quietly to revise without admitting their rustiness to supervising officers. This Thames Division initiative has been widely copied throughout the Metropolitan Police Service. The Training Unit even sells its courses to other Forces and marine organisations, markets its skills to outside agencies, and runs several winter classes in the various R.Y.A. certificates for weekend amateur sailors. 'Grotty yachty' was at one time a dismissive term aimed by a few old Thames coppers – who knew only the ways of the commercial tideway – at any keen newcomer who admitted to enjoying small boats off-duty. Nowadays it helps if officers play as well as work with boats.

Messing about in other people's boats is a profitable business for thieving river rats. Up to 50,000 craft a year are either stolen, broken into or vandalised on the Thames. Padlocks are severed with bolt-cutters and cabins rifled; brand new outboard motors, some worth thousands of pounds, are snatched from mountings; or, if that is too difficult, the entire transom may be sliced away with a power saw. Much of this stolen stuff is sold through boat jumbles, the marine equivalent of boot fairs. So in 1991 a Marine Intelligence Team (M.I.T.) was established. It is a crime squad, consisting of one Sergeant and four P.C.s (one of whom is attached to the National Crime Intelligence Service and Interpol), which concentrates upon marine theft, theft of jet skis and wetbikes, and intelligence gathering.

A laid-up cruiser stolen in winter may not be missed by its owner until Easter; so, by the time the loss is reported, a boat taken from the U.K. can have turned up in a Mediterranean marina. In 1992, to reach out beyond London's river, the M.I.T. devised a computer database called Mariner. Details of missing craft and their equipment are inserted under 65 headings, any number of which may be searched, so that duty controllers can answer queries about them arising elsewhere from sightings, stops, searches or arrests by Metpol officers and other Constabularies, or from agencies such as insurance and marine loss adjusters. They can even be contacted via the Internet. Repaint a stolen vessel, give it another name, change its equipment and even its silhouette; yet Mariner can come up with a match by original colour of upholstery, or perhaps some out-of-sight dents and scratches which only the real owner knows. The M.I.T. can tell dealers, auctioneers and private punters if the boat they are being invited to buy or sell is truly owned by the person putting it on the market, or warn

59. *Thames Division stand at the 1993 Earls Court boat show.*

them if it is not. Using the programme they have made many arrests and six-figure recoveries of property.

Visitors to recent London International Boat Shows at Earls Court have had the chance to chat with officers on the Thames Division stand about river safety, marine crime prevention, including Thameswatch (similar to Neighbourhood Watch), and Boatmark, a national boat identification database which can also be used to register expensive on-board equipment such as radios and satellite navigation equipment.

Solitary thief-takers are now rare. It is the era of the team, squad and inter-agency collaboration. On 23 November 1992, a two-year intelligence-gathering and surveillance operation culminated at Cory's barge roads, in Woolwich Reach, where a

60. *Earls Court 1996, promoting the national boat identification scheme (boat mark).*

61. *The recovery of a floating corpse can be an awkward, often gruesome task with a real risk of infection.*

62. *The drug smuggling vessel Foxtrot Five in Police custody at her moorings.*

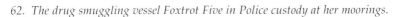

63. *The royal yacht H.M.S. Britannia, leaving the Upper Pool, on her way downriver past Thames Division's workshops and H.Q. (centre of picture).*

64. H.M.S. Britannia with Thames Police escort.

300-ton Panamanian registered vessel was unloading a nondescript cargo in black plastic bags. She was a former oil rig supply vessel, the *Foxtrot Five*, newly arrived in the Port of London from the Caribbean island of Aruba off the mainland of Venezuela. Tracked across the Atlantic by military aircraft, she had been spotted in the South Western Approaches and kept in view by long range Customs cutters using radar and other optical aids. For the ship was a drug smuggler.

At 8.25 am a raiding party of two dozen men from the Metropolitan Police SO19 Special Unit combined with the R.N. Special Boat Squadron (black-clad, in balaclava helmets and armed with semi-automatic weapons) raced up through the Thames Barrage in two fast inflatables. Thames Division boats secured the river reach, helicopters hovered overhead, as the boarding party swarmed onto the ship. At the same time Police and Customs officers on the south shore were watching a Ford Transit van containing the off-loaded cargo, as it left Valdez Wharf, and they tailed it to the Orion Business Centre at Surrey Canal Road in the New Cross district of London. Ramming open the warehouse door with a fork-lift truck, they seized over a tonne of cocaine. Worth at least £160 million, it was then the largest and most valuable drugs haul in Britain. The operation, codenamed Emerge, led to the arrest of five Britons and a Spaniard. It was a major setback for any drug traffickers with the notion that the River Thames was an unwatched way into the streets of London. The combined efforts of Thames Division, Special Branch and H.M. Customs & Excise, with H.M. Immigration officers, to intercept all foreign ships inbound has resulted in a

65. The rigid inflatable boats (R.I.B.s) of the 1990s provide a rapid rescue response.

number of such offences being detected. This multi-agency approach is how major crime is now tackled.

An increasingly familiar sight on London's thoroughfares is the Marine Incident Response Vehicle. On 24-hour emergency standby, the 2.5 turbo-diesel 400 Series Leyland-Daf van is designed and built to enable Thames officers to work away from the river, adding their expertise to that of the other emergency services. It is loaded with floodlights, ladders, rescue and body recovery equipment, radio and mobile telephones, and even has room for an inflatable dinghy. This vehicle and the command vessel *Patrick Colquhoun* were busy on 9 February 1996, after the I.R.A. bombed South Quay in Docklands, killing two people and causing more than £100 million of damage. While other units sorted out the landside mayhem, their crews searched the surface of the West India Dock for possible casualties (and the U.S.U. explored the bottom).

CHAPTER TWENTY-FIVE

Next

"The crime rate and other policing problems of the River Thames, and the resources allocated to deal with them, has to be considered in relation to the overall situation throughout the Metropolitan Police District in order that an equitable distribution of manpower and resources can be maintained."

(Assistant Commissioner W.H. Gibson, 1978)

The present day realities of running public services with the taxpayer's money have changed some of the thinking and the language of New Scotland Yard. 'Value for Money' needs to be demonstrated and priorities set. The title 'Metropolitan Police Service' reflects the need to be conscious of the public as *customers* on whose behalf there has come to be generated a *performance culture*. A charter sets out response times and other targets which are then measured and recorded to demonstrate sensitivity to the need to give good public service.

Given the challenge to all parts of the Metropolitan Police to justify their value, it is not surprising that questions have been raised about how Thames Division does its job and why it exists. It has no statutory or other written mandate for many of the roles it has created for itself; the Port of London no longer traffics in the riches of an Empire; all but a few of the capital's taxpayers, who expect the Home Office to protect them from car thieves, vandals, burglars, muggers and rapists, live and work ashore – as do their predators.

And those very Thames officers who – steeped in river lore and skilled in boat-handling – represented many of the Division's admirable traditions, were ironically also the ones who created this lack of confidence. Remote from police work ashore, they had lost touch with current administrative and policing strategies and perspectives. To them, a smart duty boat swinging on a mooring buoy was a valuable resource (and, incidentally, a useful pointer to which way the tide was flowing). Their equally dedicated, but harder-headed 1990s successors, posted in from land divisions and departments, saw the same boat more realistically as an unjustifiably idle item of equipment to be redeployed, mothballed or sold. Older Thames officers might take pride too in a boat propelled by a single screw, since it required greater skill and experience to manoeuvre in the tideway, whereas the incomers saw more sense in a twin-screw craft less demanding of a coxswain and more forgiving of any error of judgement. This clash of cultures echoed the earlier Metropolitan Police takeover of the Marine Police in 1839.

66. *The leisure scene at Wapping in 1995. The cruise ship Hanseatic is being towed from the Port, while a smaller sightseeing launch returns its tourists to the Tower.*

Of course, no cost-benefit analysis can realistically assess all the work of Thames Division. Lives saved, bodies recovered, craft salvaged, these can be added up and expressed in cash terms; but the value of preventing crime and preserving public tranquillity is incalculable. Abolish Thames Division and an inaccessible lawless zone would be created, cutting the Metropolitan Police District in half from West to East, a limbo up to half a mile wide and 54 miles long (with twice that length of shoreline). It would quickly become obvious why the River Police was formed in the first place; but, with the officers and their boats gone, it might never be re-created. Such doubts and uncertainties are not new. John Harriott rebutted them thus:

> "The supervision was so complete and systematic, and yet carried out with such an entire absence of display, that anyone looking at the surface of things might imagine the Police were more ornamental than useful. But there was not a thing went on but they knew of it, and not a man had business or carried on any calling but he was known to the Police."

More specific justification is readily found. London is still this country's busiest port with 11% of the nation's trade goods passing through its riverside wharves. The river is increasingly used for leisure, with as many as thirty large cruise ships each year visiting the special moorings provided for them in central London, while St Katharine's Dock and South Dock Marinas are tourist attractions. The Port of London Authority and the Port Health Authority are just two of several river bodies who benefit from informal contracts – known as

Memoranda of Understanding – with Thames Division, recognising by such partnerships the invaluable nature of a river police back-up to their own endeavours.

Six million visitors a year go sightseeing in over a hundred Thames pleasure boats with liquor licences, and Police are called to an average of one disturbance a week as a consequence, while the collision between the *Marchioness* and the *Bowbelle* was a shocking reminder of how badly things can go wrong out on the tideway.

The I.R.A.'s frustrated attempt to detonate two massive Semtex bombs under Hammersmith Bridge at 10.54 pm on 25 April 1996 – the third time, incidentally, since 1939 that bridge has been a target – brought the spectre of terrorist carnage and chaos back to the river. A week earlier 2,000 angry trawlermen invaded central London and made their way to the Houses of Parliament, where (joined by Tory Euro-rebels) they protested against the E.U. fishing policy; while eight trawlers anchored in the Port of London and a flotilla of smaller craft then motored to Westminster to back up the fishermen ashore. One way or another, London's waterside remains a political arena.

The booming market in affordable boats is producing a multitude of fun seekers, unaware of the river's treacherous nature, prey also to its villains. They must be protected and – insurance investigators confirm – only Police river patrols counteract the expensive kinds of mishaps and crimes to which weekend sailors are prone.

67. *Sir Peter Imbert, Commissioner of Police for the Metropolis, meeting officers of Thames Division who were on duty on the night of the Marchioness disaster in 1989.*

68. Thames Police at Hammersmith Bridge following the I.R.A. attempt to explode 30-40 lbs of Semtex in the vicinity at 10.54 pm on 25 April 1996.

At the Old Bailey in 1993, a mother who had hurled her two-year-old daughter into the Thames from Westminster Bridge was acquitted of attempted murder, but deemed insane. The child was rescued by the river police. At least forty would-be suicides are saved every year and a great many of the Royal Humane Society's reports throughout the nineteenth and twentieth centuries concern awards to Thames police officers for saving and resuscitating individuals who would otherwise have drowned. Quite apart from which Thames Division's C.I.D. was investigating six murders when it was disbanded in 1975. Between the Aprils of 1994 and 1995, Thames Division's records show:

River accidents................................	60
Crime reports..................................	182
Persons rescued (by Police)............	172
Persons rescued (by public)...........	32
Persons at risk given assistance.....	1086
Advice given....................................	2145
Vessels assisted................................	556
Dangers to navigation.....................	426
Disturbances on disco boats...........	51
Verbal warnings...............................	953
Vessels stopped...............................	796
Vessels searched..............................	245
Miscellaneous incidents..................	4888
Attempted suicides..........................	111
Bodies recovered.............................	31

69. *One of the second generation of R.I.B.s being used by Thames Division. The Pacific 24, shown above, is made by Halmatic of Southampton.*

During the same busy year, 225 of the Division's crews policed 140 river events which included: 65 regattas or races; Royalty protection and VIP security for *HMS Britannia* (57 days, 24 hours a day); four days of centenary celebrations for Tower Bridge; a State Visit; seven firework displays; the tenth anniversary of the Thames Barrage; and New Year's Eve revelries.

There is cross-party Parliamentary agreement to make more use of the tideway for both commerce and pleasure, with the first signs of renewed investment showing in the Jubilee line, East London line and Docklands Light Railway extensions and the possible high-speed Channel Tunnel rail link. London City Airport, too, concentrates business development in Dockland. Then there is the East Thames Corridor – an area a few miles either side of the Thames, from Docklands to the Medway Towns – containing 4,000 hectares for development. Easy access has resulted from the Elizabeth II Bridge crossing for the M25 at Dartford. A Department of the Environment consultation paper in April 1993 stated:

"It is clear that the East Thames area represents a course of great potential for the future of London and the South East...."

An integral element of the proposed regeneration of the East London Corridor is the Millennium Commission's decision to stage its £400 million celebratory Exhibition on the Greenwich peninsula. It is intended to resuscitate this waste land close to central London, to attract twenty million visitors – rivalling the

70. *A body has ebbed dry and a skilled team must capture the forensic scene before the river returns.*

Hyde Park exposition of 1851 and the 1951 Festival of Britain – and to be the greatest millennial event in Europe. This will be a major public order commitment for Police, much of it afloat, as tourists and sightseers are brought to the site by a fleet of river buses.

Thames Division survived the Service Restructuring of 1993-4 and, after a period of uncertainty, on 5 February 1996 became part of a new Operational Command Unit (O.C.U.) called Specialist Support, along with helicopters and dogs. At first sight a curious amalgam, the O.C.U. is a team well fitted for combined operations against such large scale crime as the importation of drugs and other maritime special operations. The Division contributes - over and above its general capability and equipment – the unique expertise of its Divisional Investigating Officer, Marine Intelligence Team and Underwater Search Unit.

Thames officers may also be co-opted into a Special Operations Team (S.O.T.) which unites officers (who are familiar with marine matters) of other divisions, law enforcement agencies and miscellaneous special units. The S.O.T. is always on call to undertake surveillance, intelligence profiles, pursuit, fast response intercepts, high access ropework infiltration, and to assist firearms teams. Far removed from the soldier-of-fortune style of macho antics that a few concerned observers may at first have feared, maritime special operations is merely the disciplined civil element for an emergency response – previously often executed by the military (who were not trained to secure evidence for any subsequent court hearings) – to high risk situations in marine environments.

New twin-screw patrol boats and a second generation of high-speed R.I.B.s are now anticipated. Meantime, officers are experimenting with a 12-hour shift working pattern, which enables them to reach the furthest limits of their patrol areas in a single duty period. The scheme is monitored by Chief Inspector Tom Pine, who also signalled a radical approach to policing the upriver reaches when he observed:

"Our response time in dealing with an incident in that area was ridiculous. It could take up to an hour for a craft to get there from the base at Shepperton and, when it did arrive, it had to do so at four miles per hour to avoid causing damage to the embankment from the wash."

To bring response times down to within twelve minutes (and so comply with the Police Charter) the innovative plan is to use two road vehicles – one a short wheelbase Landrover with Police markings, the other an unmarked general purpose car – to patrol routinely around marinas, boat yards and public places alongside the Thames. In an emergency crews will drive to boats strategically berthed along the river, including a 13-foot Dell Quay dory with an outboard motor, or use an inflatable dinghy carried in the Landrover. The construction of a Thames Division base at Richmond Lock is also planned.

Colquhoun defined his Marine Police aims and objectives as:

"....the Preservation of the Privileges of Innocence; and the Renovation of the Morals and Habits of the present and future Generations engaged in nautical Pursuits on the River Thames."

Two hundred years later, Scotland Yard drafted the following as the core purpose of the Thames Division:

(i) To uphold the common purpose and values of the Metropolitan Police Service;

(ii) To provide a specialist marine service which ensures the preservation of life and protection of people, property and the environment of the River Thames in London;

(iii) To provide marine support wherever required as an integral part of the Metropolitan Police Service;

This means that Thames Division must match the business plans, intelligence-led policies, devolved leadership and plain value-for-money approach of the remainder of the Metropolitan Police Service to combat terrorism, detect and reduce crime, and improve public reassurance through visible and effective patrolling and problem-solving. And they are doing so, with integrity, fairness and justice for all. London, the South-East and the whole country can remain proud of their expert boat-bobbies who, after two centuries, still dutifully police the river beat.

Roll of Honour

Officers killed on duty or active service
(dates of death published in Police Orders)

Thames Marine Establishment
Gabriel Franks, Master Lumper; *shot dead on duty, 16 Oct 1798*
Abraham Brown, Waterman Constable; *killed at Wapping 20 Aug 1813*
Mark Arnold, Waterman Constable; *drowned on duty 4 Jan 1820*

Thames Division, Metropolitan Police
Francis Holder, P.C. 93 TA; *drowned on duty 23 Oct 1866*
George Brooks, Inspector; *drowned on duty 16 Jun 1872*
William Robson, Inspector; *crushed on duty, 16 Oct 1884*
James Newbold, P.C. 139 TA; *drowned on duty 8 Oct 1901*
James Wheatley, P.C. 122 TA; *drowned on duty 24 June 1903*
George Spooner, P.S. 27 TA; *drowned on duty 10 Jan 1913*

By enemy action (First World War):
*Herbert Cottingham, P.C. 136 TA; *Royal Navy 10 Oct 1914*
*William Harland, P.C. 150 TA; *Royal Navy 10 Oct 1914*
*Alexander Rudd, P.C. 122 TA; *Royal Navy 10 Oct 1914*
Edmund A. Ellis, P.C. 188 TA; *Royal Navy 30 Oct 1914*
Charles A. Rayner, P.C. 85 TA; *Royal Navy 30 Oct 1914*
**Arthur Kelly, P.C. 202 TA; *Royal Navy 27 Nov 1914*
**Herbert J. Wray, P.C. 145 TA; *Royal Navy 27 Nov 1914*
Herbert C. Turtle, P.C. 217 TA; *R.L.I. 7 Apr 1915*
Joseph B. Hammond, P.C. 99 TA; *Imperial Yeomanry 3 Sep 1916*
John W. Lomas, P.C. 170 TA; *Royal Navy 31 Oct 1918*

Thames Division, Metropolitan Police
William Ware, P.C. 104 TA; *drowned on duty 6 Apr 1931*
Frederick Parnacutt, S.P.S. 8 TA; *drowned on duty 10 Nov 1937*
Albert Taylor, P.C. 59 TA; *drowned on duty 10 Nov 1937*

By enemy action (Second World War):

E.G. Dove, P.C. (War Reserve); *by air raid, on duty, 28 Jul 1941*
Charles V.C. Gould, P.C. Thames; *Royal Air Force 30 Oct 1942*
Alfred G. Bloxsome, P.S. 23 TA; *Royal Navy 6 Dec 1943*
Bertram G. Davis, P.S. 6 TA; *Royal Air Force 20 Oct 1944*
Geoffrey Richards, P.S. 33 TA; *Royal Navy 23 Dec 1944*
James W. Moore, P.C. 168 TA; *Royal Air Force 13 Jul 1945*

Thames Division, Metropolitan Police

Dennis E. Cowell, P.C. 151 TA; *drowned on duty 21 Nov 1965*
Mark A. Peers, P.C. 170 TA; *drowned on duty 15 Feb 1989*

*The deaths of these three men are remarkable because they perished together on 22 September 1914, when the obsolete British armoured cruiser *Aboukir* went down with her sister ships *Hogue* and *Cressy*, a total loss of 62 officers and 1,397 men, sunk before breakfast in less than an hour by a single German U-boat.

**Similarly, these two men were both killed on 1 November 1914, aboard the Royal Navy's cruiser *Good Hope* at the Battle of Coronel, when their ship blew up with her Admiral and all hands lost.

Officers in charge of London's River Police

The Marine Police
from 2 July 1798 to 31 August 1839

M. Armstrong, Chief Surveyor: *2 July 1798 to 2 July 1800*

John Gotty, Chief Surveyor: *2 July 1800 to 6 July 1821*

§James Evans, Chief Surveyor: *6 July 1821 to 31 Aug 1839*

Thames Division, Metropolitan Police
from 1 September 1839

§*James Evans, Superintendent: *1 Sept 1839 to 26 Oct 1848*

*J.C. Evans (Jnr), Superintendent: *30 Oct 1848 to 8 Nov 1869*

W. Alstin, Superintendent: *4 Jun 1872 to 6 Jun 1883*

G.F. Steed, Superintendent: *7 Jun 1883 to 9 Nov 1887*

G. Skeats, Superintendent: *10 Nov 1887 to 19 Sep 1891*

C. Chisholm, Superintendent: *20 Nov 1891 to 1 Aug 1899*

W.C. Robinson, Superintendent: *10 Aug 1899 to 17 May 1903*

J.W. Olive, Superintendent: *18 May 1903 to 28 May 1905*

W. French, Superintendent: *27 Jun 1905 to 30 Apr 1908*

A.G. Sutherland, Superintendent: *1 May 1908 to 17 Mar 1909*

J. Mann, Superintendent: *18 Mar 1909 to 14 Oct 1917*

¶C.A.E. Bastable , Superintendent: *17 Oct 1917 to 20 Dec 1917*

C.G. Glass, Superintendent: *21 Dec 1917 to 3 May 1920*

C.R. Clark, Superintendent: *31 May 1920 to 30 Apr 1921*

J.W. Orton, Superintendent: *1 May 1921 to 31 May 1927*

W.S. Cudmore, Superintendent: *1 Jun 1927 to 2 Apr 1928*

T.W. Faulkner, Superintendent: *6 Apr 1928 to 31 Aug 1931*

H. Dalton, Chief Inspector: *1 Sep 1931 to 3 Dec 1933*

J. Brown, Chief Inspector: *4 Dec 1933 to 23 Jan 1938*

W. Hughes, Chief Inspector: *24 Jan 1938 to 8 Feb 1940*

H.C. Hill, Superintendent: *19 Feb 1940 to 30 Aug 1942*

T. Fallon, Chief Superintendent: *31 Aug 1942 to 22 Feb 1948*

W.C. Batson, Chief Superintendent: *1 Mar 1948 to 7 Jan 1953*

A.C. Evans, Chief Superintendent: *9 Jan 1953 to 26 Mar 1954*

C.L. McDonough, Chief Superintendent: *26 Mar 1954 to 28 Feb 1962*

T. Wilkinson, Chief Superintendent: *19 Mar 1962 to 2 Mar 1965*
D. Davies, Chief Superintendent: *8 Mar 1965 to 30 Jun 1973*
H. Whittick, Chief Superintendent: *30 Jun 1973 to 7 May 1974*
G.D. McLean, Chief Superintendent: *20 May 1974 to 12 Jul 1975*
D. Hunt, Chief Superintendent: *20 Jul 1975 to 1 Jul 1976*
S.D. Pleece, Chief Superintendent: *1 Jul 1976 to 20 Nov 1978*
S. Harrold, Superintendent: *21 Nov 1978 to 14 Jul 1981*
**M.E. Allen, Superintendent: *7 Sep 1981 to 15 Jul 1990*
R.J. Glen, Superintendent: *21 Aug 1990 to 14 Mar 1995*
D. McDonald, Superintendent: *6 Mar 1995 to 3 Mar 1996*
Phil Gaisford, Chief Superintendent: *5 Feb 1996 to the present*

§   Longest serving officer (27 years, 3 months, 20 days)
*   Father and son
¶   Shortest serving officer (2 months, 3 days)
**   Longest this century

Superintendent Ronald Henry Main does not feature in this list because his period as divisional second-in-command coincided with the reign of Chief Superintendents. He holds the record for longest twentieth-century service, however, having joined in 1933 and retired on 2 May 1972 after 39 years service, almost all of it in Thames Division.

Further Reading

(in date order of publication)

Colquhoun, P: *A Treatise on the Police of the Metropolis* (5th edition, London, 1797).

The Times newspaper: 7 July, 26 July, 17 October 1798.

Colquhoun, P: *A Treatise on the Commerce and Police of the Metropolis* (London, 1800).

Harriott, John: *Struggles Through Life*, (Vols 1-III, 3rd edition, London, 1815).

Illustrated London News, 31 January 1846.

Mayhew, Henry: *London Labour and the London Poor* (1851).

The Boy's Own Paper, 'Out with the Thames Police' (*pp*75-76, 103 and 131-132, *c*.1890).

The Strand Magazine, 'A Night with the Thames Police' (*pp*124-32, 1894).

Dickens, Charles (jnr): *Dictionary of the Thames* (1895).

Dictionary of National Biography.

The Motor Boat, 'The Boats and Work of the Thames River Police' (*pp*123-125, 12 Aug 1921, *pp*161-163, 19 Aug 1921); also 'Motor Boats in the Thames Police Force' (1 June 1928).

Bowen, Frank C: *London Ship Types* (1938).

Savill, Mervyn: *Tide of London – A Study of London & its River* (1951).

Gaselee & Son Ltd: *River Thames Wharf Directory* (1954).

Richardson, Anthony: *Nick of the River* (1955).

Fallon, Tom: *The River Police* (1956).

Brief History of Thames Division, (Metropolitan Police publicity material, undated).

Thames Police Association: *Thames Police Journal* (1961 to the present).

Wright, R.M.D: *River Beat* (1966, unpublished monograph in the Thames Police Museum, Wapping).

Sheldon, Sheila M: *The Marine Police* (1968, unpublished monograph in the Thames Police Museum, Wapping).

The Grand Panorama of London – from the Thames, reproduced from the original 1844 engraving (1972).

Doxat, John: *The Living Thames – The Restoration of a Great Tidal River* (1977).

Desmond, Kevin: *The Guinness Book of Motorboating* (1979).

Anderson, Jo: *Anchor and Hope* (1980).

Bates, L.M: *The Spirit of London's River* (1980).

Cracknell, Basil E: *Portrait of London River* (1980).

Martin, Frank: *Rogues' River – Crime on the River Thames in the Eighteenth Century* (1983).

Croad, Stephen: *London's Bridges* (1983).

Weinreb, Ben, and Hibbert, Christopher: *The London Encyclopaedia* (1983).

Hardwicke, Glyn: *Keepers of the Door* (privately published *c*.1985).

Cohen, Ben: *The Thames 1580-1980, a General Bibliography* (1985).

Bunke, John: *From Rattle to Radio* (1988).

Ellmers, Chris and Werner, Alex: *London's Lost Riverscape – A Photographic Panorama* (1988).

Weightman, Gavin: *London River: the Thames story* (1990).

Leapman, Michael: *London's River* (1991).

Regan, Geoffrey: *The Guinness Book of Naval Blunders* (1993).

Joslin, John: Miscellaneous unpublished notes at the Thames Police Museum, Wapping.

Lines, Danny: Miscellaneous unpublished notes at the Thames Police Museum, Wapping.

INDEX
Asterisks indicate illustrations.